Fashionable Clothing from the Sears Catalogs

Early 1980s

Tina Skinner

Schiffer Publishing Ltd ®

4880 Lower Valley Road, Atglen, PA 19310 USA

Images used in this book are from the Sears Catalogs © Sears, Roebuck and Co., and are used with permission.

SPRING/SUMMER 1974
Pages: 6-8, 19, 22-24, 27-28, 35, 39-40, 50, 67, 69-70, 73, 75, 79-80, 90, 99, 104-105, 110, 116-118, 123-125, 127, 130, 139, 142, 158

FALL/WINTER 1974
Pages: 8-9, 22-23, 28-30, 38, 53, 60, 68-70, 74-75, 81-83, 86-87, 91, 94, 100, 110-112, 128, 143, 147-149, 151, 153

SPRING/SUMMER 1975
Pages: 10-11, 19-20, 24, 30-31, 40, 42-43, 54-55, 60, 68, 70-71, 76, 83-84, 89, 100, 102-103, 106-107, 112, 118-120, 123, 128, 130-132, 143-145

FALL/WINTER 1975
Pages: 11-14, 20, 25, 43-44, 60-61, 67, 72, 76, 81, 85-87, 92-93, 95, 103, 113, 133-134, 140, 144, 151, 154-156, 159

SPRING/SUMMER 1976
Pages: 14-15, 21, 26, 32, 34-36, 38, 45-47, 57-59, 62-63, 72, 74, 77, 81-82, 85-86, 89, 96-97, 108-109, 113-115, 120, 122, 125, 134-136, 141, 152, 156, 160

FALL/WINTER 1976
Pages: 16-18, 26, 32, 48-49, 51, 59, 63-66, 72, 78, 93, 97-98, 114-115, 124, 126, 137-138, 141, 152, 156-157, 160

Copyright © 1999 by Schiffer Publishing Ltd.
Library of Congress Catalog Card Number: 99-61170

Designed by Bonnie M. Hensley
Type set in Brochure/Aldine 721 BT

ISBN:0-7643-0876-9
Printed in China
1 2 3 4

Acknowledgments

Many thanks to Robyn Stoltzfus and Tammy Ward for their help on this and all the books in the Sears fashion series. Their assistance with the photography and organization is deeply appreciated.

Published by Schiffer Publishing Ltd.
4880 Lower Valley Road Atglen, PA 19310
Phone: (610) 593-1777; Fax: (610) 593-2002 E-mail: Schifferbk@aol.com
Please visit our web site catalog at **www.schifferbooks.com**

In Europe, Schiffer books are distributed by Bushwood Books
6 Marksbury Avenue Kew Gardens Surrey TW9 4JF England
Phone: 44 (0)181 392-8585; Fax: 44 (0)181 392-9876 E-mail: Bushwd@aol.com

This book may be purchased from the publisher. Include $3.95 for shipping. Please try your bookstore first.
We are interested in hearing from authors with book ideas on related subjects. You may write for a free printed catalog.

Contents

Introduction

I live in a college town, where thrift stores thrive. Recently I was digging through the racks in one of these establishments when I overheard two college girls shopping nearby. They were looking for costumes for an '80s party, and the one girl commented that anything tight would do.

I'm afraid they were a little off base on that, basing their choices on what might make them most popular at the party rather than reflecting the true trends of the 1980s. Still, it started me thinking about how I might dress myself if I wanted to evoke that era.

Though there was a certain shedding of innocence at the time, with suggestive lingerie and evocative evening dresses debuting in the Sears catalog, the overall fashion statement of the decade was preppy. It was a timid time for the couture world, poised between the riotous colors of the previous decade and the rebellious explosion of punk in the mid-1980s. Preppy was the sought-after image, and "dress for success" was the decade's fashion jingle. A knock-off British safari look, or a toned-down cowboy ensemble were about as bold as it got. There was some fancy stitching for the back pockets of snug, straight-leg jeans, and those still clinging to the past decade might don a flowery muu-muu or fringed jean shorts. However, you were far more likely to encounter plain blue sweaters with puffy shoulders, knee-length skirts cut along the most conservative A-lines, and a pair of argyle socks peeking out below. Diagonal stripes crossing the front panels of dresses and casual tops were about as wild as it got for the newly created Preppy. The push was for professional polish in day-to-day wear, though a jacket could be stripped away to reveal bare shoulders for a night on the town.

On the other hand, the home front was becoming quieter, with lounge wear dressed way down. From the fancy hostess gowns of the 1970s, home-wear for the 1980s was, well, more homely. Jane Fonda was bringing her workout into the home, and the ballerina leotard look for exercising was morphing into colorful separates for aerobics. Moreover, women's sportswear was beginning to resemble men's, with an evolving line of co-ed knitwear for the ever popular pursuits of jogging and tennis, but mostly just for lounging around the home.

Despite increased emphasis on fitness, the American public was expanding. Sears, too, expanded, growing from the 3-4 pages offered in the late 1970s to the full eleven pages in their spring/summer 1980 catalog dedicated to the "Medium to heavy frame and fuller, more mature figure."

In sports, our heroes on the court were John McEnroe, Bjorn Borg, Martina Navratilova, and Chris Evert. We were also marvelling at Hulk Hogan and Mr. T, two early personalities in professional wrestling.

On the home court, electronic TV tennis was making way for Pac Man technology. On the big screen, we were entranced by *Raiders of the Lost Ark*, *Ghandi*, and *Terms of Endearment*. *Chariots of Fire* told a story from the 1924 Olympics, and helped the nation recover from its disappointment after President Jimmy Carter boycotted the 1980 Summer Olympics in Moscow. That same year, the nation elected a hawk over a dove, and, in 1981, Ronald Reagan took office and helped to define the decade, ushering in the Strategic Defense Initiative and the age of "Star Wars."

Using this Book

For the fashion historian and costumer, this book offers a wonderful sampling of clothing. It documents what people wore at work, at home, and on the town. It chronicles what children wore in imitation of the big people, and what big people wore in imitation of sports stars and super models. This is a precise gauge of the fashion standards for the early 1980s.

For the collector, this book offers the original prices, rounded to the nearest dollar or half dollar, as well as an average value, for items, never worn or in perfect condition, on today's vintage and resale market. Today the thrift shops are packed with castaways from the early 1980s, and the value of these items is negligible. Many of these items are hardly worth the cloth they're made of today. The narrow-shouldered blazers and ruffled blouses congest many a rack in thrift shops, and high-end vintage stores won't touch them.

Still, these items are guaranteed to increase in value, especially when we pass into the next millennium. So it's a wide open field for the pioneer collector, willing to invest in the price of today's rags for tomorrow's potential riches.

Career Clothing

Dress Code

America's changing culture was reflected in the sales pitches of the Sears catalog, with catch phrases such as "smart investment," "handbag strategy," "perfect merger," "working day and night," and "success starts with a stunning. . . ."

T-shirt dress, pullover style with front button-placket, polyester knit, $17 [$5-10] Two-piece dress, elastic waist, $22 [$5-10] Spring/summer 1980

Spliced-front dress, spun polyester, $22 [$5-10] Tucked-front dress with piping, $20 [$5-10] Jacket dress, polyester/rayon in linen look, $30 [$5-10] Spring/summer 1982

The Accessories
Jewelry sold on page 153;
red and white belts on page 147

"Ten O'Clock Meeting," black and white jacket-dress of pique-textured polyester knit, $29 [$10-15] "On schedule" black and white stripes, $25 [$5-10] "Detailed Assignment," black dress with obi sash belt and piping, $35 [$5-10] "White Collar Works" in double layer on black and white dot-printed dress, polyester/rayon, $37 [$5-10] "Lunch Break," in woven checks with double collar and bow-tie, $37 [$15-25] Spring/summer 1983

6

P.R. Donovan

Corduroy dress, cotton/polyester, $46 [$10-20] Black classic pantsuit with lined jacket, tailored pants, $50 [$45-60] Camel and navy check dress, $34 [$5-10] Polyester pinstripe dress, $32 [$30-40] Fall/winter 1983

Dolman sleeve dress, polyester, $30 [$10-15] Multi-colored stripe dress with scoop neck, $25 [$5-10] White and gray tuck-front dress with vest, $36 [$25-35] Gray pantsuit with black velvet collar, $48 [$20-30] Fall/winter 1983

Opposite page:
Right: Wool blends from P.R. Donovan's. Bold plaid or gentle plaid, $84 each [$10-20] Fall/winter 1983

The Jacket Dress

"The versatile jacket dress . . . is a slim camisole dress with fitted jacket that goes non-stop from day to evening," polyester crepe, $36 [$35-45] Spring/summer 1980

Jacket dress of polyester knit, with pleated skirt, two-tone belt, $27 [$15-25] Spring/summer 1981

The jacket-dress, smooth knit polyester, elastic waistband, elasticized belt, $30 [$25-35] Spring/summer 1980

Button-front jumper, suede-look polyester knit, $25 [$15-25] Suede-look jacket and plaid polyester-knit dress, $36 [$5-15] Fall/winter 1981

Striped jacket-dress, black and white, of polyester/cotton jersey, $32 [$30-40] Three-piece suit-dress of polyester knit, $40 [$25-35] Dot-print dress of semi-sheer polyester/cotton voile, $28 [$10-15] Spring/summer 1982

Jacket dress of tweed-textured polyester and acrylic, $38 [$10-20] Fall/winter 1982

"Gabardine on the Go. Jacket dressing moves easily from desk to dinner." Blue with red and blue bodice, $90 [$5-15] "Busy agenda welcomes three parts that work together or go their separate ways." $82 [$5-15] Spring/summer 1983

Aqua green jacket and white polyester knit dress, $39 [$25-35] "Perfect Merger." Black and white jacket, skirt, and bodice, $47 [$15-25] Spring/summer 1983

Pencil-stripe dress, $36 [$15-25] Bow-tied jacket dress, $46 [$30-40] Fall/winter 1983

"The dress and the little white jacket." Bow-tie or V-neck dress, plus jacket, $28 [$15-25] Spring/summer 1983

11

Diagonally-striped dress with jacket, $26 [$10-15] Pleated dress with jacket, $32 [$10-15] Dress fashioned with dots and dash, $24 [$5-10] Patent vinyl belt, $8 [$2-5] "Career Bag," polyurethane, $19 [$5-15] Fall/winter 1983

FASHION NOW
The skirtsuits

Boxy jacket, straight skirt, polyester knit, $22 [$30-40] Piped jacket, straight skirt, $25 [$20-30] Spring/summer 1980

Blazer jacket, pleated skirt, $30 [$30-40] Spring/summer 1980

Suits Her

The checked shirt is sold on page 52

Oxford-weave separates, polyester/cotton blend. Blazer, $35 [$10-15] Pants with set-on waistband, zip-fly front, $16 [$20-25] Slim skirt with back zipper, $16 [$5-10] Striped knit top, $15 [$10-15] Spring/summer 1980

"The slender suit." Textured double-knit polyester in ivory with black piping or black with ivory, $29 [$10-20] Spectator pump, urethane uppers, $32 [$25-35] Spring/summer 1980

The SuperSuede™* Blazer

Team with plaid wrap-skirt and classic white-on-white shirt for a great-looking suit in separates

244 Sears ALL

SuperSuede™ blazer of triacetate and nylon, $40 [$25-35] Plaid wrap-skirt, $25 [$5-10] White-on-white shirt, $12 [$10-15] Fall/winter 1980

Pleated blouse, polyester interlock knit, $15 [$5-10]
Double-knit polyester coordinates: blazer, $32, skirt, $18, and pants, $17 [$10-20 each] Spring/ summer 1981

"Classic linen-look suit," polyester/rayon blend, $30 [$25-35] Spring/summer 1981

Jacket and pants, double-knit polyester textured with bird's-eye pique-effect, $21 [$25-35] Jacket and pleated skirt, $25 [$25-35] Spring/summer 1981

Tweed blazer, wool/polyester/acrylic, lined with rayon, $55 [$20-30] Fall/winter 1981

Textured suit, cardigan-style knit in subtle stripes or tweed, polyester/acrylic, $30 [$10-20] Satin-look bow blouse, polyester, $18 [$10-15] Fall/winter 1981

116 Sears ALL

Two-piece outfit: blazer with pants or skirt, $23 [$10-20] Knit
turtleneck dickey, $5 [$5] Fall/winter 1981

Natural tone suit by Adrianne Ross: blazer,
$34, skirt, $18, pants, $18 [$5-10 each] Floral
print blouse, $18 [$5-10] Striped V-neck
sweater vest, $16 [$5-10] Spring/summer 1982

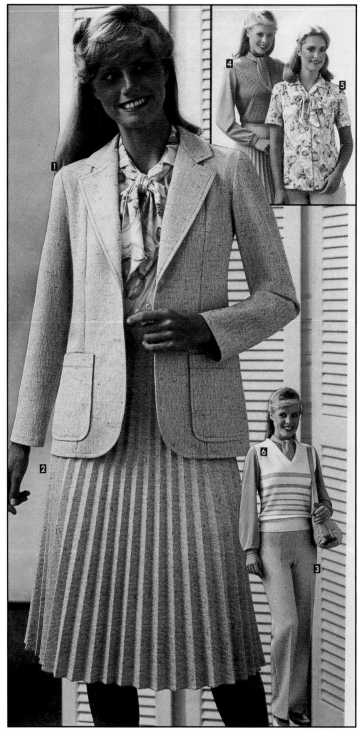

Textured Pastels

Nubby textured double-knit separates: blazer, $27, crystal-pleated skirt, $16, pants, $14, [$5-10 each] Print blouse, $15 [$5-10] Spring/summer 1982

Double-knit separates: blazer, $16, skirt, $8 [$5-10 each] Bow blouse, $10 [$5-10] Spring/summer 1982

Wool-blend flannel weave: blazer, $50, skirt, $24, pants, $26 [$15-25 each] Striped or paisley print blouse, $21 [$10-20] Fall/winter 1982

Adrianne Ross burgundy plaid separates: blazer, $37, belted skirt, $20, pants, $20 [$5-10 each] Pierrot collar blouse, $19 [$10-20] White sweater vest, $16 [$5-10] Fall/winter 1982

Tweed-textured suit, polyester/acrylic double-knit, $30 [$10-20] Striped sweater dress, $35 [$5-10] Two-piece sweater dress, $38 [$10-20] Fall/winter 1982

Three-piece suit of softly textured polyester, rayon, and silk, $120 [$70-85] Two-piece suit of polyester, rayon, and silk, $90 [$30-40] Spring/summer 1983

Polyester suit looks like smooth gabardine, $80 [$20-30] Designer-look suit in polyester/rayon blend, $75 [$30-40] Spring/summer 1983

"Good business sense means a beige poplin pantsuit of woven polyester," $51 [$25-35] "Make an investment in a classic jacket and shirt ensemble" of polyester, $38 [$15-25] Spring/summer 1983

Blue plaid blazer, $38, skirt, $22, and pants, $21 [$5-15 each] Polyester blouse, $22 [$5-10] Sweater vest, $22 [$5-10] Spring/summer 1983

Linen-look blazer, $27, front-pleated skirt, $15, pants, $17 [$5-15 each] Floral-print blouse, polyester, $14 [$5-10] Solid shirt, $12 [$5-10] Spring/summer 1983

Reefer wool coat, satin lining, $165 [$85-110] Wool-blend two-piece suit, $125 [$40-50] Fall/winter 1983

Working Separately

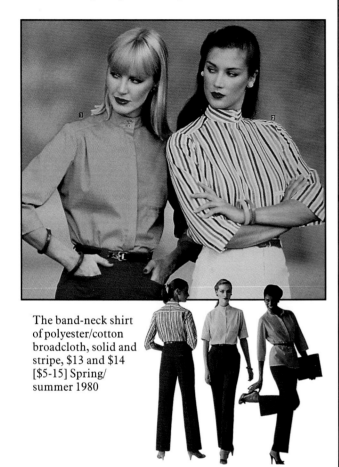

The band-neck shirt of polyester/cotton broadcloth, solid and stripe, $13 and $14 [$5-15] Spring/summer 1980

Double-knit polyester blazer, $24 [$5-10] Skirt, $17 [$5-10] Pants, $14 [$5-10] Coordinating cherry red blouse, $14 [$5-15] Print tunic, $17 [$5-10] Spring/summer 1980

GREAT MIX-ABOUTS
in flag colors

ALL Sears 53

Sears 89

Pantsuit with multi-colored print top and pull-on pants, $18 [$5-15] Two-piece dress, polyester knit, $18 [$5-15] Spring/summer 1980

226 Sears ALL

Corduroy blazer, $35 [$5-15] Jacquard sweater, $18 [$10-20] Fall/winter 1980

Ruffled blouse, $21 [$5-15] Pullover sweater, $18 [$5-10] Crystal-pleated skirt, $27 [$5-10]
Fall/winter 1980

Sweater blazer,
$32 [$10-15]
Crystal-pleated
skirt, $27 [$5-10]
Fall/winter 1980

Wide-wale
corduroy pants,
$22 [$25-35]
Button-front skirt,
$19 [$5-15] Fall/
winter 1980

24

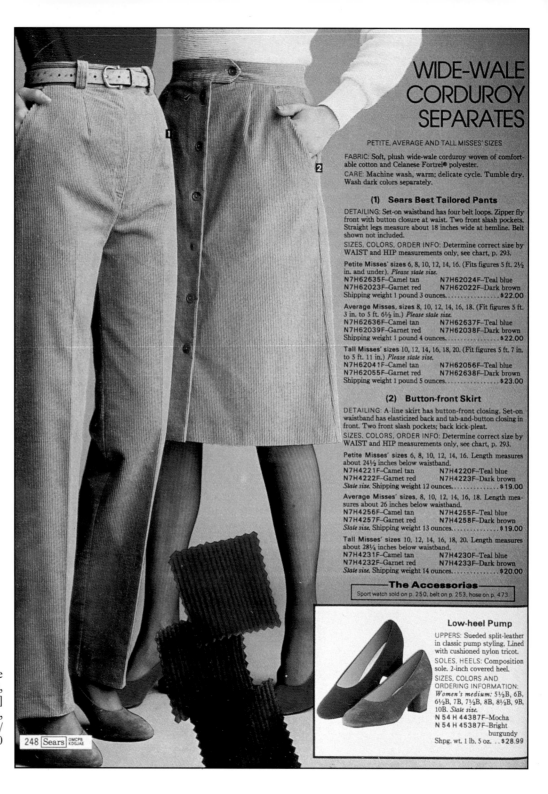

WIDE-WALE CORDUROY SEPARATES

PETITE, AVERAGE AND TALL MISSES' SIZES

FABRIC: Soft, plush wide-wale corduroy woven of comfortable cotton and Celanese Fortrel® polyester.
CARE: Machine wash, warm; delicate cycle. Tumble dry. Wash dark colors separately.

(1) Sears Best Tailored Pants

DETAILING: Set-on waistband has four belt loops. Zipper fly front with button closure at waist. Two front slash pockets. Straight legs measure about 18 inches wide at hemline. Belt shown not included.
SIZES, COLORS, ORDER INFO: Determine correct size by WAIST and HIP measurements only, see chart, p. 293.

Petite Misses' sizes 6, 8, 10, 12, 14, 16. (Fits figures 5 ft. 2½ in. and under). *Please state size.*
N7H62635F–Camel tan   N7H62024F–Teal blue
N7H62023F–Garnet red   N7H62022F–Dark brown
Shipping weight 1 pound 3 ounces.................**$22.00**

Average Misses, sizes 8, 10, 12, 14, 16, 18. (Fit figures 5 ft. 3 in. to 5 ft. 6½ in.) *Please state size.*
N7H62636F–Camel tan   N7H62637F–Teal blue
N7H62039F–Garnet red   N7H62038F–Dark brown
Shipping weight 1 pound 4 ounces.................**$22.00**

Tall Misses' sizes 10, 12, 14, 16, 18, 20. (Fit figures 5 ft. 7 in. to 5 ft. 11 in.) *Please state size.*
N7H62041F–Camel tan   N7H62056F–Teal blue
N7H62055F–Garnet red   N7H62638F–Dark brown
Shipping weight 1 pound 5 ounces.................**$23.00**

(2) Button-front Skirt

DETAILING: A-line skirt has button-front closing. Set-on waistband has elasticized back and tab-and-button closing in front. Two front slash pockets; back kick-pleat.
SIZES, COLORS, ORDER INFO: Determine correct size by WAIST and HIP measurements only, see chart, p. 293.

Petite Misses' sizes 6, 8, 10, 12, 14, 16. Length measures about 24½ inches below waistband.
N7H4221F–Camel tan   N7H4220F–Teal blue
N7H4222F–Garnet red   N7H4223F–Dark brown
State size. Shipping weight 12 ounces.............. **$19.00**

Average Misses' sizes, 8, 10, 12, 14, 16, 18. Length measures about 26 inches below waistband.
N7H4256F–Camel tan   N7H4255F–Teal blue
N7H4257F–Garnet red   N7H4258F–Dark brown
State size. Shipping weight 13 ounces.............. **$19.00**

Tall Misses' sizes 10, 12, 14, 16, 18, 20. Length measures about 28¼ inches below waistband.
N7H4231F–Camel tan   N7H4230F–Teal blue
N7H4232F–Garnet red   N7H4233F–Dark brown
State size. Shipping weight 14 ounces.............. **$20.00**

The Accessories
Sport watch sold on p. 250; belt on p. 253; hose on p. 473.

Low-heel Pump
UPPERS: Sueded split-leather in classic pump styling. Lined with cushioned nylon tricot.
SOLES, HEELS: Composition sole. 2-inch covered heel.
SIZES, COLORS AND ORDERING INFORMATION:
Women's medium: 5½B, 6B, 6½B, 7B, 7½B, 8B, 8½B, 9B, 10B. *State size.*
N 54 H 44387F–Mocha
N 54 H 45387F–Bright
                    burgundy
Shpg. wt. 1 lb. 5 oz. **$28.99**

248 Sears OMCPB KDGJAE

Corduroy blazer in three rustic shades, $35 [$5-15]

Velveteen blazer, cotton, $40 [$15-25] Wool-blend plaid skirt, $20 [$5-15] Pleated bow-tie shirt, $15 [$5-15] Fall/winter 1981

25

GOLDEN
TOUCH-SUEDE™
Teamed up with a Wool
Blend Skirt, Ruffled Blouse
and Argyle Sweater

Polyester with the look and feel of suede:
fully lined blazer, $40 [$20-30] Dirndl skirt,
$19 [$5-10] Wool-blend plaid skirt, $20 [$5-
15] Ruffled blouse, $16 [$5-15] Argyle
sweater, $18 [$5-10] Fall/winter 1981

3-piece Wardrobe

BLAZER, PANTS
AND SKIRT

$35 Average Misses' sizes

TALL MISSES' AND HALF SIZES
PRICED HIGHER

FABRIC: Smooth, supple double-knit. Jacket,
pants and red plaid skirt are 100% polyester.
Taupe plaid skirt is a blend of polyester and
acrylic.
DETAILING:
Jacket. Fitted blazer style with shaped seams
in front. Front closure has gold-color metal
"blazer" buttons. Two patch pockets; long
sleeves. Blouse and turtleneck sweater not included . . . blouse sold below; turtleneck
sweater sold on page 111.
Pants. Pull-on style with elasticized waistband.
Straight-cut legs about 19 in. wide at hem.
Skirt. Pull-on style with elasticized waistband;
pleating all around.
CARE: Machine wash, warm, delicate cycle;
drip dry.
SIZES. COLORS AND ORDER INFO:

Average Misses' sizes 8, 10, 12, 14, 16, 18, 20.
(Fit 5 ft. 3 in. to 5 ft. 6½ in.) *State size.*
T 31 G 35216F—Black; red plaid skirt
T 31 G 35266F—Taupe; taupe plaid skirt
Shipping wt. 2 lbs. $35.00

Tall Misses' sizes 12T, 14T, 16T, 18T, 20T,
22T. (Fit 5 ft. 7 in. to 5 ft. 11 in.) *State size.*
T 31 G 35217F—Black; red plaid skirt
T 31 G 35267F—Taupe; taupe plaid skirt
Shipping wt. 2 lbs. 3 oz. $37.00

Half sizes 14½, 16½, 18½, 20½, 22½, 24½.
(Fit 5 ft. 4 in. and under.) *State size.*
T 31 G 35218F—Black; red plaid skirt
T 31 G 35268F—Taupe; taupe plaid skirt
Shipping wt. 2 lbs. 3 oz. $37.00

White Lace-trimmed Blouse
FABRIC: Woven of polyester and cotton.
DETAIL: Button-front. Lace trim at stand-up
collar and elasticized sleeve openings. Black
grosgrain-ribbon bow tie. Jabot . . . lace-
trimmed half-placket. Long sleeves. Shirring at
dropped front shoulders. Straight-cut hem.
CARE: Machine wash, warm; tumble dry.
SIZES. ORDER INFO: See Chart on page 66.
Misses' sizes 8, 10, 12, 14, 16, 18. *State size.*
T 7 G 64771F—Shpg. wt. 6 oz. $15.00
Women's sizes 38, 40, 42, 44. *State size.*
T 7 G 64772F—Shpg. wt. 6 oz. $17.00

OMCKP
8GAEJD [Sears] 113

Three-piece wardrobe, blazer, pants, and skirt
of double-knit polyester, $35 [$15-30] White
lace-trimmed blouse, $15 [$5-15] Fall/winter
1981

(3) Also in
Tall Misses'
sizes

Sueded pigskin blazer with rayon
lining, $120 [$50-75] Fall/winter 1981

Blouses in "two distinctive styles with feminine accents," $14 each [$5-15]
Spring/summer 1982

"Classic items that add up to a wardrobe,"
woven blends of polyester, rayon, and flax.
Blazer, $40, trouser-style pants, $24, polka-dot
blouse, $18, polka-dot skirt, $18 [$5-15 each]
Spring/summer 1982

essentially
separate

Classic items
that add up
to a wardrobe

Convertible Jacket . . . . collar can be worn two ways

26 Sears ALL

Opposite page:

Top left: Bow blouse, $15 [$5-15] Wrap skirt, $15 [$5-10] Pipe-trimmed shirt, $15 [$5-10] Checked skirt with belt, $17 [$5-15] Convertible jacket can be worn with notched collar or Mandarin style, $26 [$15-25] Spring/summer 1982

Bottom left: "Two romantically ruffled sweaters" of acrylic and nylon, $18 each [$5-10 each] Fall/winter 1982

Right: Textured sweater dressing with knit separates. Scoop-neck sweater, split skirt, sweater with capelet, $20, and pleated skirt, $20 each [$5-10 each] Fall/winter 1982

Left: Oxford cloth shirt with Mandarin collar, solid or striped, $15 [$5-15] Fall/winter 1982

Right: "Day to dusk dressing." Dress in two-tones of gray in fluid polyester crepe de chine has bateau neckline, $72 [$10-20] Silksatonal® dressing, polyester, $76 [$5-15] Spring/summer 1983

ALL Sears 55

"Fashions that work: 8 mixable pieces." Silk/polyester blend, $12-30 each [$5-20 each]
Spring/summer 1983

Style's in the bag
With our vibrant toppers
and our "paper-bag waist"
style bottoms

"Vibrant toppers." Polyester blend blouses, $18 each [$5-15] Spring/summer 1983

Opposite page:
Left: Woven polyester blouse, $15
[$5-15] Spring/summer 1983

Bright pink polyester dress piped in blue, $29 [$5-10] Striped T-top and split skirt, polyester/rayon poplin, $29 [$5-15] Spring/summer 1983

Velvet blazer, cotton with rayon lining, $40 [$20-30] Wool-blend flannel, $50 [$20-30] Fall/winter 1983

Smooth woven blouse, $20 [$5-15] Wool-blend pants, $24 [$15-25] Wool-blend skirt, $22 [$5-10] Textured sweater vest, $18 [$5-10] Fall/winter 1983

Pleated-front blouse, $20 [$5-15] Skirts in rich fall colors, $20 [$5-15] Fall/winter 1983

Oxford cloth shirts, $14 [$5-15] Fall/winter 1983

Woven blazer, lined, Perma-prest® polyester gabardine, $40 [$5-15] Fall/winter 1983

Pinstripe three-piece suit, woven polyester, $85 [$30-45] Fall/winter 1980

Wrinkle-resistant polyester double-knit separates: blazers and sportscoats, $40-45 [$15-20] Reversible vests, $16 [$5-10] Coordinated slacks, $17 [$15-25] Spring/summer 1980

Comfortable, versatile
CORDUROY

ALSO IN TALL, SHORT

Three-piece corduroy suit, $75 [$70-80]
Sportcoat, $40 [$35-45] Fall/winter 1980

CONTEMPORARY

Tweed and corduroy blazers, $50 [$35-45] and slacks, $23 [$20-30]
Fall/winter 1980

ALSO IN SHORT, TALL, EXTRA TALL, BIG, BIG-TALL

DOUBLE-KNIT SEPARATES
Versatile wardrobe expanders
. . . order each piece
in the size you need,
in the colors you want

Double-knit separates: blazer, $45 [$15-20] reversible vest, $17
[$5-10] slacks, $18 [$15-25] Spring/summer 1982

35

Authentic Indian madras blazers, 100 percent cotton, $65 [$35-45] Stretch-woven polyester/cotton slacks, $22 [$15-25] Spring/summer 1982

Blazers
ALSO IN
SHORT,
TALL

Stretch-woven polyester separates: blazer, $75 [$15-20] reversible vest, $24 [$5-10]
coordinated slacks, $30 [$15-25] Spring/summer 1983

Levi's® finely tailored corduroy separates:
blazer, $75 [$45-65] vest, $21 [$10-20]
slacks, $30 [$35-45] Fall/winter 1983

Wool herringbone sportcoat, $95 [$15-20]
Fall/winter 1983

ALSO IN
SHORT
TALL
EXTRA TALL
BIG
BIG-TALL

Dressing Up

Appliqued dress with wide belt, polyester, $26 [$10-20] Spring/summer 1980

Fashion shirring, smooth-knit polyester, $24 [$5-10] Plastic choker and matching earrings, $9 [$5-10] Spring/summer 1980

Piped wrap dress, $30 [$5-10] Spring/summer 1980

Black jacket and print dress, smooth-knit polyester, $22 [$5-15] Piped jacket and dress, $23 [$5-15] Spring/summer 1980

The Knotted-vamp Slide

UPPERS: Smooth leather-look urethane with knotted vamp.
SOLES, HEELS: Polyurethane unit bottom with rounded toe. Insole cushioned at heel. Tapered heel is 3¾ inches high.
SIZES. COLORS. ORDER INFO: *Women's medium sizes:* 5B, 6B, 7B, 8B, 9B, 10B. *Please state full size as listed. Half sizes order ½ size larger.*
N54K44348F–Pale beige
N54K45348F–Raspberry pink
Shpg. wt. 1 lb. 2 oz. $23.99

Hair Picks

Plastic hair pick with matching-color plastic flower and contrasting-color leaves. About 4 in. long. Set of 2 in same colors.
COLORS AND ORDERING INFO:
T88 K 8358–Red; yellow
T88 K 8359–Royal blue; hot pink
Shpg. wt. set 1 oz. . . . . .set $4.00

ALL Sears 85

V-neck dress, $15 [$5-10] Boat-neck dress, $15 [$5-10] Spring/summer 1980

39

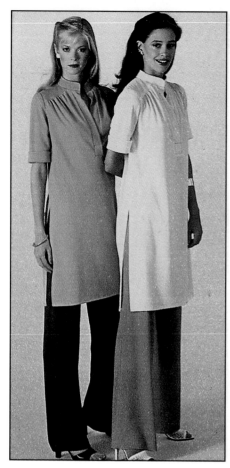

Double-knit polyester pullover, $20
[$5-10] Spring/summer 1980

Dress with contrast piping, $21
[$5-10] Spring/summer 1980

Full-skirted dress, double-knit polyester, in print or solid
coral or amber, $20 [$5-10] Spring/summer 1980

"Bodywear for all occasions." Classic-style leotard with spaghetti straps, $10 [$5-10] Straight-leg pants, $15.50 [$5-10] Wrap-around skirt, $17 [$5-10] Wet-look leotard with spaghetti straps, $15 [$5-10] Spring/summer 1980

All sweaters in the same six colors

Turtleneck sweater, soft acrylic, $13 [$10-15] Crew-neck sweater, $13 [$10-15] Suede-look two-tone belt, $8 [$5-10] Fall/winter 1980

Blouse with stand-up collar, $13 [$10-20]
Blouse with V-neckline, $12 [$5-10] Fall/
winter 1980

Velour

Bateau-neck Dress
PETITE, AVERAGE AND
TALL MISSES' SIZES

FABRIC: Velour . . . a velvety knit of Arnel®
triacetate and nylon.
DETAILING: Pullover style has a bateau
neckline. Long, slim sleeves. Elasticized
waistline with shirring. Matching patent
vinyl belt cinches the waist; has a pull-
through prong buckle. Thin braid trim pipes
neckline and armholes.
CARE: Machine wash at warm temperature;
line dry or tumble dry.
SIZES, COLORS, ORDERING INFORMATION:
Determine correct size by BUST measure-
ment only, see chart on page 342.
Petite Misses' sizes 6P, 8P, 10P, 12P, 14P.
(Fit figures 5 feet 2½ inches and under.)
Please state correct size.
N 31 H 6562F—Garnet red
N 31 H 6565F—Black
N 31 H 6569F—Medium rose
N 31 H 6563F—Aqua blue
N 31 H 6567F—Lavender
Shipping weight 15 ounces $32.00
Average Misses' sizes 8, 10, 12, 14, 16, 18.
(Fit figures 5 feet 3 inches to 5 feet 6½
inches.) *Please state correct size.*
N 31 H 6624F—Garnet red
N 31 H 6627F—Black
N 31 H 6631F—Medium rose
N 31 H 6625F—Aqua blue
N 31 H 6629F—Lavender
Shipping weight 1 pound $32.00
Tall Misses' sizes 10T, 12T, 14T, 16T,
18T, 20T. (Fit figures 5 feet 7 inches to 5 feet
11 inches.) *Please state correct size.*
N 31 H 6724F—Garnet red
N 31 H 6727F—Black
N 31 H 6731F—Medium rose
N 31 H 6725F—Aqua blue
N 31 H 6729F—Lavender
Shipping weight 1 pound 2 ounces . . .$34.00

330 Sears OMCP8 KDGJAE

Velour bateau-neck dress, $32 [$10-20]
Fall/winter 1980

Quilted jacket-dress, $28 [$20-30]
Fall/winter 1980

The Petite Miss

Good fit is good fashion. That's why we're proud to present a size range just for you! Every petite selection is specially proportioned. Because that's the secret of good fit.

THESE STYLES ALSO AVAILABLE IN AVERAGE MISSES' SIZES

Look for other Petite Misses' apparel throughout our fashion section

1

The Shoe
UPPERS: Urethane. Vamp urethane lined. Adj. strap; buckle. Imported. SOLES, HEELS: Insole; cushioned heel pad. Composition sole. 3¼-in. heel.
SIZES, COLORS AND ORDERING INFO:
Women's med. sizes: 5½B, 6B, 6½B, 7B, 7½B, 8B, 8½B, 9B and 10B. *State size.*
N 54 H 45151F—Medium gray
N 54 H 43351F—Black
N 54 H 45251F—Magenta
N 54 H 45451F—Teal blue
Shipping weight 1 lb. 1 oz......$28.99
332 [Sears] ALL 2

Full-skirted print dress, polyester knit, $22 [$5-10] Fall/winter 1980

Bouclé-textured acrylic knit sweater, $28 [$5-15] Spring/summer 1981

Jersey wrap-tie dress, polyester, $30 [$5-10] Spring/summer 1981

[Sears] 153

Two-piece border print dress, polyester/wool blend, $30 [$5-15] Calico-print dress, polyester, $24 [$5-10] Fall/winter 1981

Ruffled dress, $29 [$5-10] Dress with suede-look vest, $34 [$5-15] Fall/winter 1981

Dressy knit crepes, polyester: ruffle-trimmed pantsuit, $31 [$5-15] two-tone surplice dress, $26 [$5-10] Fall/winter 1981

Soft Challis

Romantic Prints in a Victorian Mood

ALSO JUNIOR SIZES

(1 thru 3)
CARE: Machine wash, warm; tumble dry
. . . item (1) with similar colors.

(1) Two-piece Border Print Dress
FABRIC: Soft, woven blend of polyester
and wool. Delicate multicolor print of mini-
roses on a dark green ground.
DETAILING:
Top. Front button closing. Small notched
collar; drop front shoulderline; long sleeves
with one-button cuffs. Straight-cut hemline
. . . to wear in or out.
Skirt. Set-on waistband has back zipper
closing; softly gathered all around.
SIZES AND ORDERING INFO:
Junior sizes 5, 7, 9, 11, 13, 15. (Fit 5 ft. 2 in.
to 5 ft. 6 in.) *State size.*
T 19 G 1938F—Wt. 7 oz. $30.00
Petite Misses' sizes 6P, 8P, 10P, 12P, 14P,
16P. (Fit 5 ft. 2½ in. and under.) *State size.*
T 31 G 70205F—Wt. 10 oz. $30.00
Average Misses' sizes 8, 10, 12, 14, 16, 18.
(Fit 5 ft. 3 in. to 5 ft. 6½ in.) *State size.*
T 31 G 70206F—Wt. 11 oz. $30.00

(2) Calico Print Dress
FABRIC: Woven polyester. Calico floral
print in lilac on navy blue ground.
DETAILING: Pullover style. Round neck-
line has front slit with loop-and-button
closing; deep yoke in front and back. The
neckline, yoke and elasticized wrists of the
long sleeves are ruffled trimmed. Self-fabric
tie belt is included . . . to wear or not.
SIZES AND ORDERING INFO:
Junior sizes 3, 5, 7, 9, 11, 13, 15. (Fit 5 ft. 2
in. to 5 ft. 6 in.) *State size.*
T 19 G 1940F—Wt. 7 oz. $24.00
Petite Misses' sizes 6P, 8P, 10P, 12P, 14P.
(Fit 5 ft. 2½ in. and under.) *State size.*
T 31 G 11395F—Wt. 10 oz. $24.00
Average Misses' sizes 8, 10, 12, 14, 16, 18.
(Fit 5 ft. 3 in. to 5 ft. 6½ in.) *State size.*
T 31 G 11396F—Wt. 11 oz. $24.00
Half sizes 14½, 16½, 18½, 20½, 22½. (Fit
5 ft. 4 in. and under.) *State size.*
T 31 G 11398F—Shpg. wt. 13 oz. $26.00

(3) Foulard Print Dress
FABRIC: Soft woven blend of polyester and
rayon. Tiny foulard print in dark brown
and green on tan ground.
DETAILING: Pullover style. Ruffled front
button-placket closing to waist. Band neck
has extensions that tie in front. Shirred
drop front shoulderline; long sleeves with
one-button cuffs. Elasticized waistline; self-
fabric tie belt.
SIZES AND ORDERING INFO:
Junior sizes 5, 7, 9, 11, 13, 15. (Fit 5 ft. 2 in.
to 5 ft. 6 in.) *State size.*
T 19 G 1939F—Wt. 7 oz. $28.00
Average Misses' sizes 8, 10, 12, 14, 16, 18.
(Fit 5 ft. 3 in. to 5 ft. 6½ in.) *State size.*
T 31 G 70306F—Wt. 11 oz. $28.00
Tall Misses' sizes 12T, 14T, 16T, 18T,
20T, 22T. (Fit 5 ft. 7 in. to 5 ft. 11 in.) *State
size when ordering.*
T 31 G 70307F—Wt. 12 oz. $30.00

ORDER YOUR USUAL SEARS SIZE. If in
doubt, see the Fitting Room: pages 101, 117.

Foulard print dress, $28 [$5-10] Fall/winter 1981

Textured sweater-knit
partners: camisole or
shell, $16 [$10-20]
cardigan, $21 [$10-20]
skirt, $22 [$10-20]
Spring/summer 1982

"Silksational® dressing . . . the polyester fabric is soft-as-silk." Surplice front dress, $79 [$5-10] Deep dolman sleeves and a touch of piping, $79 [$5-10] Fall/winter 1982

Ruffles and Romance

Polyester blouses: ruffle jabot, $15, pin tucks and ruffles, $15, and cascading capelet, $18 [$5-15 each] Fall/winter 1982

Two-tone jacket-dress with lace trim, $30 [$10-20] Ruffle-trim dress and vest, $25 [$5-10] Fall/winter 1982

Ribbonette pantsuit with sheer knit top, opaque pants, $33 [$5-15] Ribbonette jumpsuit with sheer knit jacket, $35 [$5-15] Fall/winter 1982

Diagonally tiered dress, polyester knit, $32 [$5-10] Ruffle surplice-front dress, $34 [$5-10] Fall/winter 1983

Dress with matching lace trim, $32 [$5-10] Classic shirtdress with contrasting trim, $34 [$5-10] Fall/winter 1983

Casually Attired

Fashion jeans, 100 percent cotton, in white, red, violet, royal blue, or jade green, $15 [$25-35] Spring/summer 1980

Straw fedora with grosgrain ribbon, $14 [$5-15] Stretch tube top, $5.50 [$10-15] Spring/summer 1980

Sporting separates: terry-knit long sleeve cardigan with white piping, $17 [$10-15] smooth-knit striped T-top, short sleeves, $8 [$5-10] polo-shirt, $11 [$10-15] v-neck pullover, $9 [$10-15] Spring/summer 1980

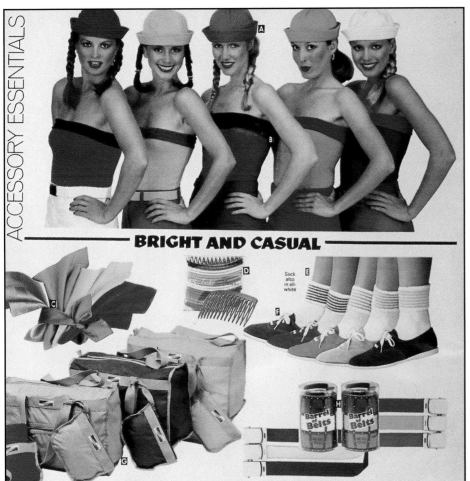

BRIGHT AND CASUAL

Sailor hat, cotton poplin, $5 [$5-15]
Cuffed terry tube top, $11 [$10-15]
Spring/summer 1980

Johnny-collar T-shirt, polyester/cotton knit, $13
[$15-20] Textured tunic of open-weave polyester/
cotton, $15 [$20-30] Terry V-neck top, $11 [$15-20]
Spring/summer 1980

"Fashion value three-piece outfit." Smooth knit polyester shirt, sleeveless pullover, and straight-cut, elasticized pants, $21 [$45-55] Spring/summer 1980

Denim-look shift with calico print trim, $11 [$20-30] Check shift with embroidered trim, $12 [$5-10] Cotton muu-muu in multi-colored screen-print, $13 [$20-30] Spring/summer 1980

TEXTURE

Smooth and rugged fabrics
...mix for the natural look

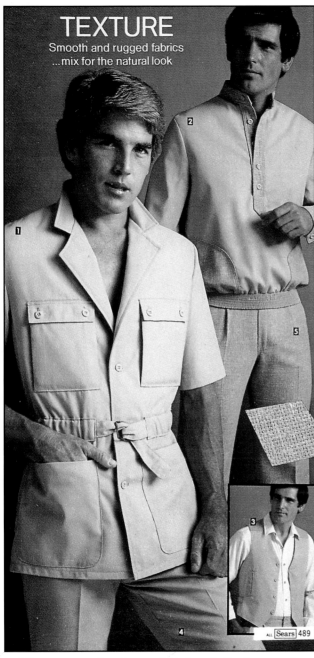

"Texture, smooth and rugged fabrics mix for the natural look." Short sleeve jacket, smooth polyester/cotton, $35 [$5-10] Long-sleeve pullover, woven polyester/cotton, $25 [$5-10] Woven slacks, $20 [$10-15] Sleeveless vest, $16 [$5-10] Spring/summer 1980

Shirts and Shorts for contemporary guys

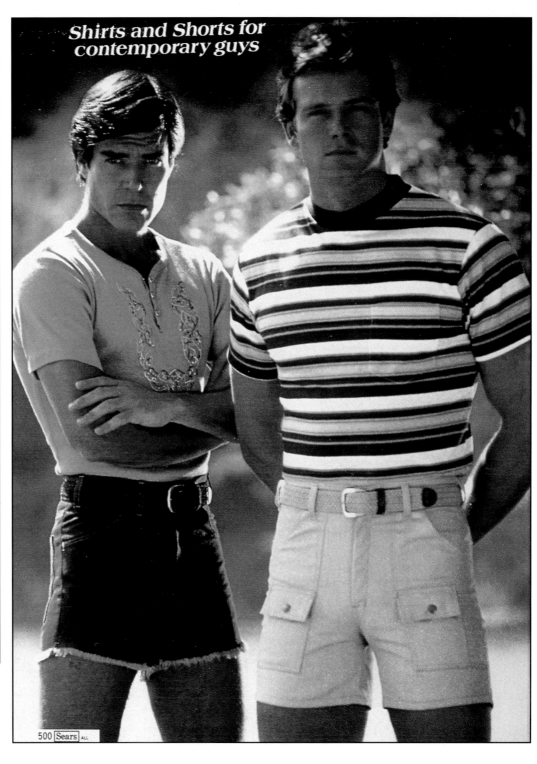

Shirt with embroidered front, $8 [$15-20] Cotton fringed denim shorts, $9 [$20-25] Striped crew-neck shirt, $5 [$15-20] Shorts with bush pockets, $10 [$20-30] Spring/summer 1980

51

(15 thru 19) PERMA-PREST® Slacks...
classic styling plus easy care

(20 thru 25) Lustrous, satin-look Shirts
featuring all-over prints

Satin-look shirts featuring all-over prints or tone-on-tone stripes, woven blend of acetate and nylon, $7 [$25-35] Fall/winter 1980

ALL Sears 253

"The country look." Brushed flannel shirt, $16 [$15-20] Brushed chino pants, $17 [$20-30] Reversible vest, $20 [$5-10] Reversible skirt, reverses to plaid, $22 [$10-20] Ostrich-look leather belt, $8 [$10-15] Fall/winter 1980

232 Sears ALL

Spliced velour top, cotton and polyester, in navy blue and red, brown and bright gold, camel tan with spruce green, or gray with purple, $21 [$15-25] Two-way stretch polyester gabardine jeans, $17 [$25-35] Fall/winter 1980

Slacks include matching belts

604 Sears ALL

Lightweight acrylic chenille knits with scoop or keyhole neckline, $15 [$20-30] Spring/summer 1981

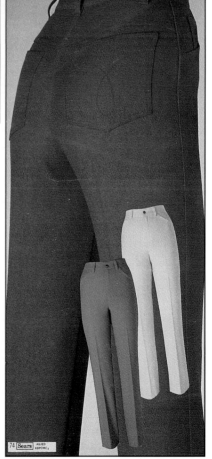

Two-way stretch woven polyester gabardine jeans, $17 [$25-35] Spring/summer 1981

Shawl-collar cardigan, acrylic/polyester/wool knit, $30 [$35-45] Flannel slacks with matching belt, $25 [$30-40] Fall/winter 1980

74 Sears

The
Textured
Shell
$10⁰⁰

Shell in lightweight acrylic scramble stitch for look of
bouclé, $10 [$10-15] Spring/summer 1981

Polyester knit dress, "a wardrobe essential," in
medium aqua green, bright red, navy blue, or pale
yellow, $19 [$5-10] Spring/summer 1981

Border print sundress and jacket, polyester/rayon
twill-weave, $26 [$10-15] Spring/summer 1981

Here Comes The Dragon . . .

"The Dragon: our symbol for quality at reasonable prices. Compare our new shirts and sweaters with any of the other well-known knits." Knit shirt, $12 [$15-20] Cardigan sweater, $20 [$20-25] Spring/summer 1981

Textured V-neck pullover, polyester terry, $9 [$5-10] Open collar polyester pullover, $10 [$15-25] Button-front shirt, polyester/cotton knit, $14 [$15-25] Spring/summer 1981

Plush velour V-neck top, $16 [$10-15] Fall/winter 1981

55

JACQUARD
PATTERNED
SWEATERS
. . . thick and warm;
cozy enough for
the chilliest weather

CABLED
VELOURS

Wool/acrylic-blend sweaters in solid, $16, or jacquard, $18 [$15-20 each] Fall/winter 1981

Jacquard patterned acrylic sweaters with snowflake or reindeer pattern, $18 [$15-20] Fall/winter 1981

White-on-white shirt of woven polyester and cotton, $12 [$10-15] Velour cabled vest, $14 [$5-10] Velour cabled top, $20 [$5-10] Fall/winter 1981

Sweater jacket, cable-knit acrylic, with button-up collar, $23, or shawl collar, $19, [$15-20 each] Fall/winter 1981

Navy

Currant red

Gray heather

Camel tan

SOFT FASHION TUNICS

(1) Challis print Tunic

FABRIC: Challis floral print fabric is made of a brushed polyester and rayon blend for a wonderfully soft, warm feel.
DETAILING: Pullover style has a stylish button mandarin collar. A center pleat extends down from the ½-placket buttonfront. Long, set-in sleeves have cuffs. The self-fabric tie sash is secured by self-fabric sash loops at waist. Straight-cut bottom.
CARE: Machine wash, warm temperature; line or tumble dry.
SIZES, COLORS, ORDERING INFO:
Misses' sizes 10, 12, 14, 16, 18 and 20. *Please state correct size.*
T 7 G 3417F—Brown floral print
T 7 G 3418F—Navy blue floral print
Shipping weight 7 ounces $15.00
Women's sizes 38, 40, 42 and 44. *Please state correct size.*
T 7 G 3433F—Brown floral print
T 7 G 3435F—Navy blue floral print
Shipping weight 7 ounces $18.00

(2) Border print Tunic

FABRIC: Soft, interlock polyester knit. The attractive all-over paisley print is accented by a larger floral border print on the bottom.
DETAIL: Pullover style has a stand-up collar and a slit front opening at neckline. Soft shirring at drop-front shoulderline. Long set-in sleeves have ruffled elasticized wrists. Straight-cut bottom.
CARE: Machine wash, warm temperature; line or tumble dry.
SIZES, COLORS, ORDERING INFO:
Misses' sizes 8, 10, 12, 14, 16, 18, 20. *Please state correct size.*
T 7 G 64751F—Navy blue print
T 7 G 64752F—Brown print
Shipping weight 6 ounces $13.00
Women's sizes 38, 40, 42, 44 and 46. *Please state correct size.*
T 7 G 64763F—Navy blue print
T 7 G 64764F—Brown print
Shipping weight 6 ounces $15.00

ORDER YOUR USUAL SEARS SIZE. If in doubt, see the Fitting Room on page 68

52 Sears ALL

Challis-print tunic of brushed polyester and rayon, $16 [$5-10] Border print tunic of interlock polyester knit, $15 [$10-20] Fall/winter 1981

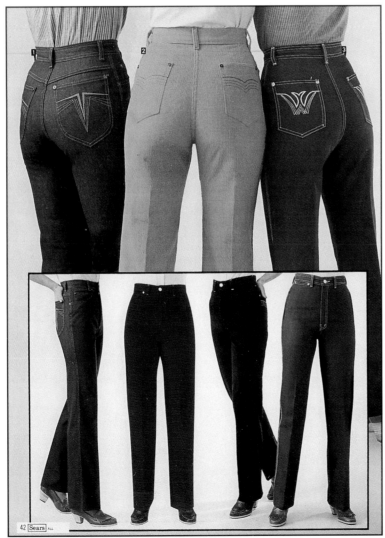

42 Sears ALL

Five-pocket denim jeans, $18 [$10-20] Three-pocket corduroy jeans, $18 [$10-20] Three-pocket denim jeans, $18 [$10-20] Fall/winter 1981

WARM
FLANNELS

. . . new looks
for old favorites

Warm flannels in button-down collar
style, $13, or pullover, $14 [$15-20 each]
Fall/winter 1981

Turtleneck sweater, rib-knit acrylic, $10 [$10-15]
Sweater vest, $14 [$5-10] Heather plaid pants,
double-knit brushed polyester, $15 [$5-10] Fall/
winter 1981

The Accessories
Shoes sold on page 86,
white watch on page 94

Striped seersucker shirt in white and khaki, blue, pink, yellow, or lilac, $13 [$10-20] Solid seersucker-look shirt, $12 [$10-20] Spring/summer 1982

34 Sears ALL

"Contemporary sports dressing." Pants with elasticized back, $23. White jacket, $34. Plaid shirt, $16. Striped Y-neck top, $14. Floral print top, $14. A-line wrap skirt, $21. Shorts with elasticized back, $12. [$5-20 each] Spring/summer 1982

Set of 2 Bandana Scarfs

Cotton scarfs measure 22 inches square and feature traditional western print and border. Set includes one red scarf and one navy scarf.

ORDERING INFORMATION:
T 88 K 8204—Shipping weight set 2 oz...Set $2.50

ALL 2 Sears 39

Terry active wear in pink, yellow, blue, white, and multi-color stripes: V-neck top, $10. Pull-on pants, $13. Polo shirt, $13. Pull-on shorts, $7. Jacket, $18. Striped crew-neck top, long sleeves, $14. [$10-25] Spring/summer 1982

"Western-look in s-t-r-e-t-c-h denim." Western-style skirt, $20 [$5-10] Western-style shirt, $20 [$5-15] Plaid shirt, $17 [$5-15] Blazer, $35 [$10-15] Pants, $22 [$15-25] Spring/summer 1982

46 Sears ALL

Our Jumpsuit that fits

. . . because of its easy-to-adjust straps and smooth-draping style

$19.99 Misses' sizes

ALL Sears 43

Striped T-top, Jersey knit polyester and cotton, $16 [$5-10] Polyester/cotton twill jumpsuit with adjustable straps, in red, khaki, or navy blue, $20 [$10-20] Spring/summer 1982

Lace-collar blouse with bright red, brown, or navy stripes, $17 [$5-10] Woven polyester/cotton cloth, $18 [$5-10] Spring/summer 1982

Safari-look separates: multi-colored print shirt, $16 [$5-15] khaki pants, $18 [$10-15] multi-color striped shirt, $16 [$5-10] khaki shorts, $12 [$15-25] Spring/summer 1982

50 Sears ALL

Left: Tiered skirt, polyester/rayon weave or 100-percent cotton, $15 [$10-20] Embroidered shirt, $13 [$1 15] Print shirt, $10 [$5-15] Spring/summer 1982

Right: Denim jacket and skirt, $38 [$10-25] Khaki jacket and folkloric print sundress, polyester and rayon, $27 [$20-30] Sleeveless wrap dress, polyester and rayon, $27 [$15-20 Print blouson dress $27 [$5-10] Tropica print camisole, $9 [$10-15] Spring/summer 1982

Short-sleeve crewneck sweatshirt with chest stripe, $15 [$10-20] Elastic-waist shorts, $14 [$5-15] Fashion-collar knit shirt, $15 [$10-20] Sweatpants with grey piping, $15 [$10-20] Baseball-style jacket, $20 [$10-20] Crewneck T-shirt, $10 [$5-15] Spring/summer 1982

Polyester/cotton poplin dress with reversible sash, $25 [$5-15] Spring/summer 1982

"Bold print" woven shirt, polyester/rayon, $14 [$20-30] Fatigue-style slacks with matching belt in natural, khaki, or olive drab, $23 [$25-35] Spring/summer 1982

Soft, acrylic/nylon sweaters in blue, rose, cream, or gray, raglan sleeves, crocheted and scalloped trim at neckline, $18 [$20-30] Fall/winter 1982

Sweater jacket of acrylic knit, $26 [$25-35] Fall/winter 1982

Mandarin collar tunic, $16 [$5-10]
Fall/winter 1982

Blouse with ruffled collar, front button opening, $19 [$10-15] Split skirt with yoke front, $24 [$5-15] Acrylic jacquard, $19, and solid-color, $21, sweaters [$15-20] Fall/winter 1982

Silk blouses in gentle floral, tonal stripes, watercolor images, or solid, $18-20 [$10-15] Spring/summer 1983

DAVID STRAUSS

Cool cotton sweaters, $16 [$5-15] Spring/summer 1983

Cotton-blend separates: diagonal striped top, $14 [$5-10] shorts, $14 [$10-15] jacket, $30 [$10-15] skirt, $20 [$5-10] dolman-sleeve top, $16 [$5-10] pants, $22 [$10-15] Spring/summer 1983

Chambray shirts of polyester/cotton weave, $16.50 [$15-25] Spring/summer 1983

The
Prairie
Look

Polyester/cotton blouses in ruffle and lace or bib yoke styles, $18-22 [$15-25] Spring/summer 1983

Polyester/cotton blouses, $17 [$15-25]
Spring/summer 1983

Styled pants of polyester/cotton, $17 [$10-15] Spring/
summer 1983

67

Classic broadcloth shirts of polyester and cotton, $8-10 [$10-20] Spring/summer 1983

"Budget Shop Zip & dash™ dresses," $15 each [$5-15] Spring/summer 1983

Cool and comfortable cotton sweaters, $12 [$10-20] Spring/summer 1983

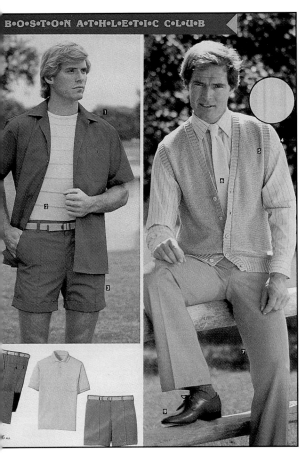

"Boston Athletic Club" cotton and cotton-blend separates. Polyester/cotton shirt, $16 [$10-20] Crewneck pullover, $14 [$10-15] Belted shorts, $17 [$10-20] Cardigan vest, $22 [$5-15] Cotton tie, $7.50 [$5-10] Belted slacks, $25 [$25-35] Spring/summer 1983

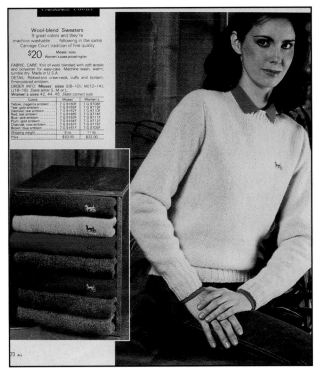

Wool-blend Sweaters
8 great colors and they're machine washable . . . following in the same Carriage Court tradition of fine quality

$20 Misses' sizes
Women's sizes priced higher

FABRIC, CARE: Knit of wool blended with soft acrylic and polyester for easy-care. Machine wash, warm; tumble dry. Made in U.S.A.
DETAIL: Ribbed-knit crew-neck, cuffs and bottom. Embroidered emblem.
ORDER INFO: Misses' sizes S(8–10); M(12–14); L(16–18). State letter S, M or L.
Women's sizes 42, 44, 46. State correct size.

Colors	Misses'	Women's
Yellow, magenta emblem	7 G 9180F	7 G 9708F
Teal, gold emblem	7 G 9165F	7 G 9713F
Oatmeal, teal emblem	7 G 9166F	7 G 9710F
Red, teal emblem	7 G 9168F	7 G 9714F
Blue, teal emblem	7 G 9183F	7 G 9711F
Plum, gold emblem	7 G 9184F	7 G 9712F
Charcoal, rose emblem	7 G 9162F	7 G 9715F
Brown, blue emblem	7 G 9181F	7 G 9709F
Shipping weight	9 oz.	11 oz.
Price	$20.00	$22.00

"All-American" wool-blend sweaters, $20 [$15-25] Fall/winter 1983

RUSTIC CHARM

Sears ✦ Best

Wrapped in fashion
. . . great for walks in the woods or shopping around town

$24 Misses' sizes
Women's sizes priced higher

FABRIC, CARE: Thick, soft shaker-knit of acrylic. Machine wash, warm; tumble dry.
DETAIL: Ribbed-knit edging.
ORDER INFO:
Misses' sizes S(8–10); M(12–14); L(16–18). State letter S, M or L.
X 7 G 9035F—Gray heather
X 7 G 9036F—Navy blue
X 7 G 9032F—Cream
X 7 G 9033F—Black
X 7 G 9031F—Green
X 7 G 9034F—Burgundy
Shipping weights 1 lb. 10 oz...$24.00
Women's sizes 42, 44, 46. State size.
X 7 G 9045F—Gray heather
X 7 G 9046F—Navy blue
X 7 G 9042F—Cream
X 7 G 9043F—Black
X 7 G 9041F—Green
X 7 G 9044F—Burgundy
Shipping weight 1 lb. 14 oz...$26.00

Fairfield Park
Corduroy Shoulder Bag
Rugged-style, roomy cotton corduroy bag has leather trim. Fabric lined. Front flap has buckle clasp. Inside zipper pocket. Outside pocket with flap. Webbed shoulder strap. Fairfield Park logo on front. Key chain. Measures about 10x3x7 vs. high.
ORDER INFO:
88 G 1511—Rust
88 G 1509—Navy blue
88 G 1510—Brown
Shpg. wt. 15 oz...............$15.00

ORDER YOUR USUAL SEARS SIZE.
If in doubt, see the Fitting Room on page 643.

24 ALL

"For walks in the woods or shopping around town," shaker-knit acrylic sweater jackets, $24 [$25-35] Fall/winter 1983

Classic argyle vest, $18 [$5-10] Argyle sweater, $20 [$5-15] Fall/winter 1983

Jacquard sweater, $20 [$15-25] Elastic-waistband twill-weave polyester skirt, $20 [$5-10]
Zipper-front vest, $20 [$5-10] Pants, $20 [$10-20] Fall/winter 1983

The SWEATSHIRTING approach to lounge dressing means style, fit and comfort

"The sweatshirting approach to lounge dressing means style, fit, and comfort." Assorted sweat sets, $18-28 [$15-30] Fall/winter 1983

Velour big top, to wear alone or with pants, $18 [$15-25] Lounge set perfect for home entertaining, $28 [$25-35] Caftan, $28 [$10-20] Fall/winter 1983

Model Clothes

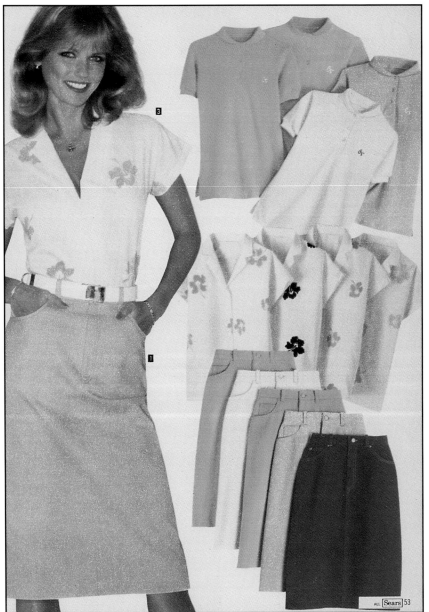

In the spring of 1981, Sears introduced a line of Cheryl Tiegs™ clothing. Here the supermodel helps push a print shirt, $12 [$10-15] Polo shirt, $14 [$10-15] Western-style skirt, $18 [$10-15] Spring/summer 1981

Classic navy blazer, wool/polyester blend with nylon lining, $55 [$30-40] Cotton denim jacket with ribbed-knit trim, $25 [$25-35] Fall/winter 1981

Tuxedo-front shirt, polyester/rayon broadcloth, $18 [$15-25] Wool-blend cabled sweater, $24 [$5-10] Corduroy trouser jeans, $25 [$20-30] Fall/winter 1981

Classic polo shirt, $16 [$10-15] Cuffed shorts, $12 [$15-25] Spring/summer 1982

Striped polo, polyester/cotton knit, $16 [$10-15]
Jeans featuring back-zip pockets, $25 [$25-35]
Spring/summer 1982

Maillot, $24 [$20-30] Spring/summer 1982

Nylon ciré jacket, $20 [$10-20] Quilted sweatshirt, $18 [$5-10] Pleated corduroy trousers, $22 [$20-30] Fall/winter 1982

Silk/acrylic-blend sweater vest, $20 [$5-10] Blouse with quilted accents, polyester weave, $20 [$10-20] Pleated wool-blend trousers, $26 [$20-30] Fall/winter 1982

Tuxedo shirt and tie and pleated front shirt, $20 each [$15-25] Wool-blend split skirt, $26 [$10-15] Fall/winter 1982

Quilted polyurethane vest, $26 [$5-10] Ruffle-front blouse, $20 [$15-20] Western-style jeans, $20 [$25-35] Fall/winter 1982

Focus on Color

Linen-look blouse of polyester and rayon, $18 [$10-15] Pleated trousers, $24 [$15-25] Spring/summer 1983

Striped polo shirt, $18 [$10-15] Cuffed shorts, $12 [$15-25] Spring/summer 1983

Swimsuit available in Regular and Full Bust sizes

24 ALL

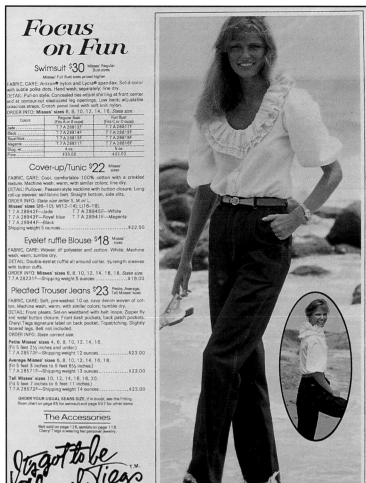

Focus on Fun

Swimsuit $30
Misses' Regular Bust sizes

Misses' Full Bust sizes priced higher

FABRIC, CARE: Antron® nylon and Lycra® spandex. Solid-color with subtle polka dots. Hand wash, separately; line dry.
DETAIL: Pull-on style. Concealed ties adjust shirring at front center and at contour-cut elasticized leg openings. Low back; adjustable crisscross straps. Crotch panel lined with soft knit nylon.
ORDER INFO: Misses' sizes 6, 8, 10, 12, 14, 16. State size.

Colors	Regular Bust (Fits A or B cups)	Full Bust (Fits C or D cups)
Jade	T 7 A 28812F	T 7 A 28817F
Black	T 7 A 28814F	T 7 A 28819F
Royal blue	T 7 A 28813F	T 7 A 28818F
Magenta	T 7 A 28811F	T 7 A 28816F
Shpg. wt.	4 oz.	5 oz.
Price	$30.00	$32.00

Cover-up/Tunic $22
Misses' sizes

FABRIC, CARE: Cool, comfortable 100% cotton with a crinkled texture. Machine wash, warm, with similar colors; line dry.
DETAIL: Pullover. Peasant-style neckline with button closure. Long roll-up sleeves; self-fabric belt. Straight bottom, side slits.
ORDER INFO: State size letter S, M or L.
Misses' sizes S(6-10); M(12-14); L(16-18).
T 7 A 28942F—Jade   T 7 A 28945F—White
T 7 A 28943F—Royal blue   T 7 A 28941F—Magenta
T 7 A 28944F—Black
Shipping weight 5 ounces....................$22.00

Eyelet ruffle Blouse $18
Misses' sizes

FABRIC, CARE: Woven of polyester and cotton. White. Machine wash, warm; tumble dry.
DETAIL: Double-eyelet ruffle all around collar. ¾-length sleeves with button cuffs.
ORDER INFO: Misses' sizes 6, 8, 10, 12, 14, 16, 18. State size.
T 7 A 28231F—Shipping weight 5 ounces........$18.00

Pleated Trouser Jeans $23
Petite, Average, Tall Misses' sizes

FABRIC, CARE: Soft, pre-washed 10 oz. navy denim woven of cotton. Machine wash, warm, with similar colors; tumble dry.
DETAIL: Front pleats. Set-on waistband with belt loops. Zipper fly and metal button closure. Front slash pockets; back patch pockets. Cheryl Tiegs signature label on back pocket. Topstitching. Slightly tapered legs. Belt not included.
ORDER INFO: State correct size.
Petite Misses' sizes 4, 6, 8, 10, 12, 14, 16.
(Fit 5 feet 2½ inches and under.)
T 7 A 28573F—Shipping weight 12 ounces..........$23.00
Average Misses' sizes 6, 8, 10, 12, 14, 16, 18.
(Fit 5 feet 3 inches to 5 feet 6½ inches.)
T 7 A 28571F—Shipping weight 13 ounces..........$23.00
Tall Misses' sizes 10, 12, 14, 16, 18, 20.
(Fit 5 feet 7 inches to 5 feet 11 inches.)
T 7 A 28572F—Shipping weight 14 ounces..........$23.00

ORDER YOUR USUAL SEARS SIZE. If in doubt, see the Fitting Room chart on page 85 for swimsuit and page 507 for other items.

The Accessories
Belt sold on page 126, sandals on page 118.
Cheryl Tiegs is wearing her personal jewelry.

It's got to be Cheryl Tiegs T.M.

Eyelet ruffle blouse, $18 [$20-30] Pleated trouser jeans, $23 [$25-35] Spring/summer 1983

Cover-up tunic, $22 [$5-10] Swimsuit of nylon and spandex, $22 [$20-30] Spring/summer 1983

Cheryl Tiegs™ for Girls. Stripe top, $10, cuffed walking shorts, $13, white top, $8, and pants with matching belt, $15 [$10-15 each] Spring/summer 1983

Cotton denim jacket, $30 [$35-45] Western jeans, $22 [$25-35] Jabot-front blouse, polyester/rayon, $22 [$15-25] Trouser skirt, $20 [$10-15] Fall/winter 1983

Soft turtleneck polyester blouse, $20 [$15-25] Tweed sweater vest, $22 [$5-10] Wool-blend trousers, $26 [$20-30] Fall/winter 1983

77

Children and Early Teens

Children's Waterproof Rainwear
FOR SIZES TO 6x.

Children's water-proof cartoon rainwear with Superman©, Popeye©, and Petticoats and Pantaloons©, $6 [$20-30] Girls' three-piece waterproof rain set, $8 [$10-15] Fall/winter 1980

Children's waterproof Cartoon Rainwear

FABRIC: Vinyl bonded to vinyl. (1 thru 3) are yellow; (4) is light blue.
DETAILING: Drawstring hood helps keep out rain and wind. Raglan sleeves, underarm vents. Heat-sealed seams. Screen print front, back. Imported. (1 thru 3) have zip front, 2 patch flap pockets. (4) has snap placket front, 2 patch pockets.
CARE: Wipe clean with a damp cloth.

SIZES. ORDER INFO: Regular size 3, 4, 5, 6, 6x.
State size. See Chart on page 66.
(1) 29 H 62031F—Superman*
(2) 29 H 62029F—Spiderman**
(3) 29 H 62032F—Popeye†
(4) 29 H 33025F—Petticoats 'n Pantaloons▲
Shipping weight 14 oz. $5.99
*©D.C. Comics. Inc.
**©Marvel Comics Group
†©King Features Syndicate. Inc. 1978
▲Design© Roth International

Plush velour two-piece sets for boys and girls, $16 [$25-35] Fall/winter 1980

Children's Winnie-the-Pooh® over-the-foot all-weather boots, $15 [$20-25] Fall/winter 1981

282 ALL

Boys nightwear. Superman© robe, $9 [$25-35] Pajamas with Superman©, Ziggy©, Snoopy®, Hulk®, Spiderman®, or Popeye®, $7-8 [$20-30] Coordinating cape, $3 [$2-5] Space print and football pajamas, $5.50 each [$10-15] Fall/winter 1980

Girls nightwear, $7-10 [$10-20] Fall/winter 1980

79

Strawberry Shortcake® nightwear, $8-9
[$20-30] Fall/winter 1982

Officially licensed NFL shirts, $6, and shorts, $5 [$5-10 each] Spring/summer 1981

Terry jumpsuit and romper with cotton striping, $13 and $10 [$15-25] Polyester/cotton nightshirt in long and short styles, $15 and $12 [$10-15] Spring/summer 1981

"Colorful T-shirts with favorite sayings and TV show prints, $4 [$5-10] camouflage fatigue-style jeans, $13 [$15-20] Character print sweatshirts with Snoopy®, Pac Man®, and The Dukes of Hazzard®, $10 [$10-15] Spring/summer 1982

From "six pages of fashions inspired by the movie Annie." Plaid blouse with Annie® buttons, $9, denim overalls, $13, twill split skirt with Annie® print, $8, Check blouse with scalloped, embroidered collar, $8, Annie®-print blouse, $8, twill pants, $10, twill jumper, $10, twill jacket, $12, sweater with embroidery, $8, and print turtleneck, $6 [$15-20 each] Fall/winter 1982

186 Sears

Classic preppy-look shirts, $9 [$5-10] Preppy-styled work pants, $12 [$5-10] Crew-neck sweaters, $7 [$10-15] Fall/winter 1980

Fun pocket jeans with Bugs Bunny® and other cartoon animals, $13 [$5-10] Fall/winter 1980

"Wisely-styled separates" coordinate owl motifs. Sunny Bunch™ shirts, $10 [$5-10] Screen-printed bib overalls, $15 [$5-10] Vest, $11 [$5-10] Jeans, $13 [$5-10] Spring/summer 1980

82

Sweater vest, $14, short-sleeve sweater shirt, $11, ribless corduroy fashion jeans, $17 [$5-10 each] Fall/winter 1980

Yellow, royal, and red color-slice knit top, $6, red knit top with Mork and Mindy™, $4, bibbed overall, $17, Mork® navy suspender pants, $17 [$5-10] Fall/winter 1980

Shoes sold on page 260

"Rugged with Style." Wide wale corduroy vest and pants, $25 [$30-40] Brushed twill plaid shirt, $11 [$10-15] Corduroy jacket, $22 [$10-15] Twill pants with bellows pockets, $13 [$5-10] Fall/winter 1983

Complementary Separates
Featuring corduroy and brushed acrylic

Especially for you from Winnie-the-Pooh

370 Sears ALL

Polyester/cotton blouses, $8 [$10-15] Corduroy overalls, $13 [$20-30] Brushed acrylic pleated jumper, $12 [$15-20] Polyester shearling-look vest, $7 [$5-10] Corduroy pants, $10 [$10-15] Fall/winter 1981

84

"All-occasion dresses for little girls," with back closures, woven polyester/cotton, $11-13 [$15-25] Spring/summer 1982

Peasant-style dress, $17, turquoise sleeveless dress with jacket, $19, smocked sundress with jacket, $16 [$5-10] Spring/summer 1982

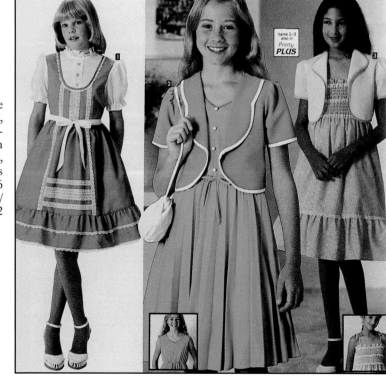

Items 2-3 also in *Pretty PLUS*

White gauze Victorian-style blouse, $14 [$20-25] Flounced denim skirt, $17 [$5-10]
Peplum blouse with appliqued flowers, $11 [$5-10] Pink pants with elastic ankles, $15, and
trouser-look pleated pants with belt, $16 [$5-10 each] Spring/summer 1982

"Sweatworks® fleeced mini dress with dolman sleeves, $18 [$5-10] Fall/winter 1983

Miss Manhattan® Blouses for Girls

"Miss Manhattan® blouses for girls," $11-13 [$5-10] Fall/winter 1983

"Versa-style suits with Lycra® spandex grow with you so the suit you love this year will fit from season to season." One size, $10 [$5-10] Spring/summer 1981

Quilt-lined Coats

Your choice $29.99 Regular sizes

PRETTY-PLUS PRICED SLIGHTLY HIGHER

Blue denim coat, beige pile coat, and blue fleece coat, $30 each [$35-45] Fall/winter 1981

Opposite page:
Left: Jersey-knit, chenille-look knit, and mesh-knit tops, $6-13 [$5-10] Wrangler® painter's cloth jeans, $14 [$10-20] Spring/summer 1980

Right: Western-style jeans, $14.50 [$20-30] Slit skirt, $15.50 [$5-10] Spring/summer 1980

Juniors and Misses

Lush velour tops in V-neck, $13 [$10-15] or V-neck with stripes and crew-neck with wide ribs, $17 [$5-10] Fall/winter 1980

Acrylic pullover sweater with jacquard patterned stripe, $18 [$15-20] Wool-blend pants, $20 [$20-30] Cardigan sweater, $19 [$20-30] Wool-blend wrap skirt, $20 [$10-15] Fall/winter 1981

Crew-neck sweater, acrylic, $23 [$20-30] Plaid shirt, $19 [$20-25] Polyurethane leather-look jacket, $33 [$30-40] Corduroy knickers, $22 [$10-20] Corduroy pants, $24 [$30-40] Fall/winter 1982

Wrangler® sweatshirt, $12 [$10-15] Wrangler® jeans, $26 [$20-30] Jeans with back bellow pockets, a "trimmer version of the baggie," $23 [$10-15] Fall/winter 1982

Multi-color pullover and pleated skirt, $18 [$15-25] Solid knit top and matching shorts with paperbag waist, $23 [$15-25] Casual smock jacket, polished twill, $30 [$5-10] Pants with paperbag waist, $24 [$10-20] Spring/summer 1983

Long jumpsuit, $24 [$25-35] Short jumpsuit, $20 [$20-25] Striped T-top, $10 [$5-10] Spring/summer 1983

89

Textured sweaters of spun and texturized polyester, $17-19 [$10-20]
Fall/winter 1983

Virgin wool sweater, $16 [$15-25]
Fall/winter 1983

JR Bazaar presents
Textured Sweaters at exceptional low prices

Overdyed (garment is stone washed then overdyed) denim vest, $26 [$5-10] Fleece sweatshirt, $14 [$5-10] Western-style overdyed denim jeans, $26 [$20-30] Overdyed chambray shirt with plaid tie, $21 [$5-10] Overdyed mini skirt, $19 [$10-20]
Fall/winter 1983

Round-collared sleeveless top in hot pink, bright yellow, blue, red, or jade green, $8 [$10-15] Solid color pull-on skirt, $12 [$5-10] Sweetheart neckline top, $9 [$15-20] Print half-circle skirt, $15 [$5-10] Spring/summer 1980

Shirt jacket, $21 [$10-15] Twill pants with elastic waistband, $19 [$10-15] Jacquard pattern sweater, $23 [$5-10] Check print skirt, $19 [$5-10] Fall/winter 1981

Vested dress of polyester and rayon, $30 [$5-10] Spring/summer 1980

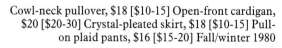

Camisole and skirt print coordinates, $14 [$15-25] Eyelet-embroidered blouse, $16 [$15-20] Knit camisole, $8 [$10-15] Medium blue pants with natural-waist, $18 [$5-10] Circle-strap sandal, urethane, $20 [$10-20] Spring/summer 1980

Cowl-neck pullover, $18 [$10-15] Open-front cardigan, $20 [$20-30] Crystal-pleated skirt, $18 [$10-15] Pull-on plaid pants, $16 [$15-20] Fall/winter 1980

Reversible quilted jacket, $25 [$5-10] Camisole top with spaghetti straps, self-lined front, $10 [$10-15] Two color double-V top, $15 [$5-10] Spliced sweatshirt style top, $15 [$5-10] Accordion pleated skirt, $17 [$10-15] Fall/winter 1980

Velour dress with shoulder button accents, side slit, $32 [$5-10] Fall/winter 1980

Polyester dresses in draped neckline, pointed collar, and V-neck styles, $20 each [$10-15] Fall/winter 1980

SHIRT DRESSING:
MADRAS-LOOK

$23

Junior, Petite Misses'
and Average Misses' sizes

FABRIC: Domestic plaid fabric with the look of madras is woven of polyester, cotton. Multicolor plaid is navy blue, pale gold, currant red.
DETAILING: Tailored pullover style is slightly shirred from front shoulder seams. Elbow length sleeves with cuffs, tab and button trim. Solid white band collar, tab and 5-button front placket, and sleeve tabs. Self-fabric vinyl-backed belt with white tab and buckle.
CARE: Machine wash, warm; tumble dry.
SIZES AND ORDER INFO: Order your usual Sears size. If in doubt, see charts on pages 150 and 151 . . . BUST measurement only.

Junior sizes 3, 5, 7, 9, 11, 13, 15. (Fit figures 5 ft. 2 in. to 5 ft. 6 in.) State size.
T 19 A 1886F—Shpg. wt. 9 oz. $23.00
Petite Misses' sizes 4P, 6P, 8P, 10P, 12P, 14P. (Fit 5 ft. 2½ in. and under.) State size.
T 31 A 1517F—Shpg. wt. 11 oz. $23.00
Average Misses' sizes 8, 10, 12, 14, 16, 18. (Fit 5 ft. 3 in. to 5 ft. 6½ in.) State size.
T 31 A 1617F—Shpg. wt. 12 oz. $23.00

The Accessories
The gold color shell earrings and silver color hoop earrings are sold on page 196.

Home Delivery makes Catalog Shopping even more convenient . . . ask for details

Sears 143

Madras-look shirt dress, $23 [$10-20] Spring/
summer 1981

Sheer polyester/cotton voile
shirtdress with jacket, $29 [$10-15]
Spring/summer 1981

144 Sears ALL

SHEER DRESSING:
FLORAL PRINTS

(1) Voile Dress with lace collar
FABRIC: Sheer voile woven of polyester and cotton. Multicolor floral print on white ground. White collar; burgundy red ribbon tie.
DETAILING: Pullover style has round lace collar; ribbon tie at slit neckline opening. Short, cap-style sleeves. Elasticized waistline with self-fabric spaghetti tie belt.
CARE: Machine wash, warm; tumble dry.
SIZES AND ORDERING INFORMATION: Order your usual Sears size. If in doubt, see Junior chart on page 150. Misses' chart on page 151 . . . BUST, WAIST and HIP measurements.
Junior sizes 3, 5, 7, 9, 11, 13, 15. (Fit figures 5 ft. 2 in. to 5 ft. 6 in.) State size.
T 19 A 1993F—Shpg. wt. 8 oz. $22.00
Petite Misses' sizes 6P, 8P, 10P, 12P, 14P. (Fit figures 5 ft. 2½ in. and under.) State size.
T 31 A 1518F—Shpg. wt. 8 oz. $22.00
Average Misses' sizes 8, 10, 12, 14, 16. (Fit figures 5 ft. 3 in. to 5 ft. 6½ in.) State size.
T 31 A 1618F—Shpg. wt. 9 oz. $22.00

(2) Knit Dress with double-V neck
FABRIC: Sheer polyester knit. Multicolor floral border print on white ground.
DETAILING: Pullover style with V-neck in both front and back. Elasticized at shoulders for shirred look. Short sleeves with slit and ties. Elasticized waistline and self-fabric tie belt. Skirt flares softly from V-shaped inserts.
CARE: Machine wash, warm; tumble dry.
SIZES AND ORDERING INFORMATION: Order your usual Sears size. If in doubt, see Junior chart on page 150. Misses' chart on page 151 . . . BUST, WAIST and HIP measurements.
Junior sizes 5, 7, 9, 11, 13, 15. (Fit figures 5 ft. 2 in. to 5 ft. 6 in.) State size.
T 19 A 1994F—Shpg. wt. 8 oz. $26.00
Petite Misses' sizes 6P, 8P, 10P, 12P, 14P. (Fit figures 5 ft. 2½ in. and under.) State size.
T 31 A 1519F—Shpg. wt. 9 oz. $26.00
Average Misses' sizes 8, 10, 12, 14, 16, 18. (Fit figures 5 ft. 3 in. to 5 ft. 6½ in.) State size.
T 31 A 1619F—Shpg. wt. 10 oz. $26.00

(3) Voile Shirtdress with Jacket
FABRIC: Dress is sheer voile woven of polyester and cotton. Multicolor floral print on beige ground. Jacket is woven of polyester and rayon with the linen-look. Solid beige color.
DETAILING: Jacket. Semi-fitted style has a notched collar and single-button front closing. Short sleeves turn back to form cuffs.
Dress. Sleeveless-style dress has button front placket with notched shirt collar. Elasticized waistline; self-fabric spaghetti tie belt.
CARE: Machine wash, warm; tumble dry.
SIZES AND ORDERING INFORMATION: Order your usual Sears size. If in doubt, see Junior chart on page 150. Misses' chart on page 151 . . . BUST, WAIST and HIP measurements.
Junior sizes 5, 7, 9, 11, 13, 15. (Fit figures 5 ft. 2 in. to 5 ft. 6 in.) State size.
T 19 A 1892F—Shpg. wt. 13 oz. $29.00
Petite Misses' sizes 4P, 6P, 8P, 10P, 12P, 14P. (Fit figures 5 ft. 2½ in. and under.) State size.
T 31 A 7542F—Shpg. wt. 13 oz. $29.00
Average Misses' sizes 8, 10, 12, 14, 16, 18. (Fit figures 5 ft. 3 in. to 5 ft. 6½ in.) State size.
T 31 A 7642F—Shpg. wt. 14 oz. $29.00

Sears 145

Sheer polyester/cotton voile dress with lace
collar, $22 [$5-10] Knit dress with double-V
neck, $26 [$5-10] Spring/summer 1981

Dress with short puff sleeves, $26, or long sheer sleeves, $27
[$15-20 each] Fall/winter 1981

Oxford pleated pants of cotton/polyester blend,
$20 [$5-10] Blazer in stripes or solid, $34 [$5-10]
Spring/summer 1982

Cool sweater dresses with ruffled
collar, $28, or scallop-edged
ribbed trim, $25 [$30-35]
Spring/summer 1982

Classic woven dresses in twin print with mock lace-up front detail, float dress with lace collar and square yoke, or lacy stand-up collar styles, $27.50 [$10-20] Fall/winter 1982

Linen-look dress with white trim, $28 [$5-10] Jacket and print dress, $38 [$5-10] Spring/summer 1982

Blouses with detachable bow, cotton/polyester broadcloth, $15 [$5-10] Jacquard sweater vest, acrylic knit, $16 [$5-10] Fall/winter 1983

Classic cotton corduroy blazer, fully lined with polyester, $36 [$10-15] Fall/winter 1983

Denim in Detail

Stretched Tight

PERMA·PREST®
STRETCH-KNIT JEANS
$11⁹⁹ Petite Misses' and Average Misses' sizes

Tall Misses' and Women's sizes Priced Higher

4

WOMENSWEAR... our special apparel section in Women's and Half sizes is on pages 110 to 121

SUPER DETAILING: Lots of white topstitching points up the western styling

COMFORTABLE STRETCH: Knit of polyester and nylon with just enough stretch for comfortable fit

ALL₂ Sears 57

The emphasis was on form, and a real snug fit in the early 1980s. Here "The Stretch Jeans" of double-knit polyester and nylon, straight legs approximately 20 inches wide at hem. $12 [$30-40] Spring/summer 1980

Stretch Denim SEPARATES

Also in **TALL EXTRA TALL**

Brushed denim separates that "stretch for comfort in action." Blazer with two buttons, inside pocket, slightly padded shoulders, full lining, $45 [$45-55] Vest with five buttons, full lining, $18 [$10-15] Jeans with slant front pockets, simulated watch pocket, $18 [$10-15] Fall/winter 1980

Western-style Blazer (1)
available in tan and blue

ROEBUCKS
for Juniors

Lycra® was becoming a common ingredient in daily life, here in spandex stretch jeans.
$25 [$20-25] Fall/winter 1982

Denim separates for men in a choice of colors: "Western blue, Contemporary blue, or
Tan." Blazer, $55 [$45-50] Vest, $22 [$10-15] Jeans, $22 [$10-15] Three-eyelet tie
Oxford, leather with vinyl lining, $35 [$30-40] Spring/summer 1982

Brand Names

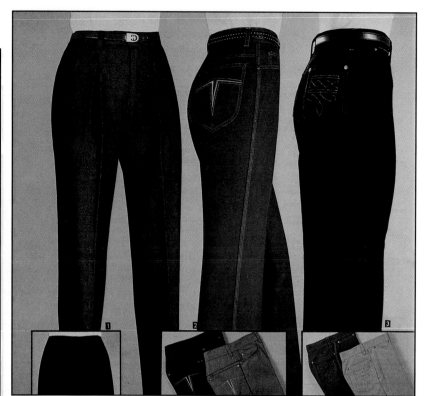

Designer jeans and escalating status prices occurred in the 1970s. In the early 1980s, dozens of companies were trying to cash in on the concept, and the benefits, with varying success. Here N'est-Ce Pas?® claims to offer the "French fit." $20 [$20-25] Fall/winter 1981

"Designer-inspired denim, twill, and corduroy jeans." $18-19 [$20-25] Fall/winter 1982

In 1982, Sears signed a boon contract with Levi's®, and the following year wrangled a deal with Wrangler®. Here, as part of a complete line of goods, are "Original Levi's® Playwear for toddlers and juveniles. Western shirts, $12 [$10-15] Western jeans, $15 [$40-50] "Koveralls," $16 [$20-25] Fall/winter 1982

Levi's® fashions for men. Denim and chambray shirts, $25 [$25-35] Western jeans, $19 [$70-80] Fall/winter 1982

Levi's® Fun Wear for girls and young juniors. Corduroy jeans, $16 [$20-25] Plaid ruffle shirt, $16 [$12-15] Tuxedo shirt, $17 [$12-15] Fall/winter 1982

Levi's® Casual Apparel for women and juniors: Levi's® Bend Over™ Western Jeans of stretch polyester, $29 [$60-70] Elastic-back brushed denim jeans, $27 [$50-60] Fall/winter 1982

"Here comes Wrangler 100% denim jeans . . . in your choice of Wrapid Transit Jeans Fit or Wrangler® for Men Mature Fit, $20-26 [$30-35] Spring/summer 1983

Special Touches

"A wardrobe essential," these "extra-long, straight legs for today's slim look" jeans were adorned with Western embroidery, $18 [$20-30] Fall/winter 1980

COTTON JEANS

Pastel-colored sheeting or navy denim . . . with the feminine touch of peekaboo lace at the back pockets

Wardrobe essentials and low-priced at

Sheeting **$17** | Denim **$19**

Cotton jeans in pastels or navy with lace pocket trim, $17-19] [$10-15] Spring/summer 1981

Denim shirtdress or coatdress, snap-front closure, front and back yokes, $24 [$40-50] Fall/winter 1980

Cowboy Appeal

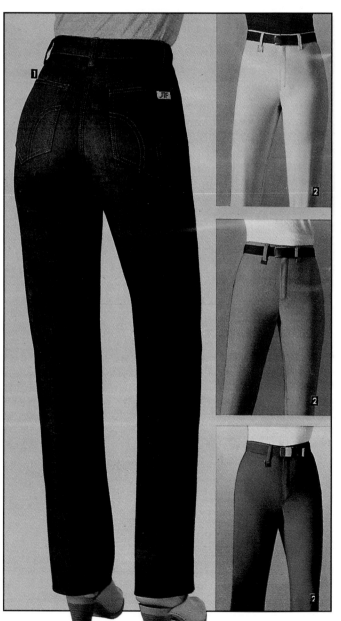

Sears has always catered to a large audience of buyers in the West, and thus Western styles have been a mainstay. In the 1980s, however, this line of clothing expanded following the popularity of the movie *Urban Cowboy*. Here Western-style jeans are modeled alongside regular denims and "s-t-r-e-t-c-h cotton jeans." $19 [$30-35] Spring/summer 1980

Both items
ALSO IN
TALL

Coat
ALSO IN
EXTRA TALL,
BIG-TALL

Rancher coat and jacket of split cowhide, polyester shearling-look lining, $115 [$80-100]
Rancher jacket, $89 [$80-100]
Fall/winter 1980

Woven Western shirts, $12 [$10-15] Suede-cloth
fringed vest, $6 [$5-10] Felt cowboy hat, $8 [$10-15]
Western canvas shoulder bag, $5 [$10-15]
Fall/winter 1981

Toppers

ROEBUCKS
AUTHENTIC WESTERN WEAR

Split cowhide fringed jacket, hers and his,
$100-110 [$150-180] Fall/winter 1980

Black

Cream

Bur-
gundy

Brown

Knit or shearling-look vest, $8 [$5-10] Suede-
look hat, $18 [$15-20] Western belt, $8 [$5-10]
Bolo tie, $4 [$3-5] Fall/winter 1981

Toughskins® indigo-look denim jeans, $11 [$10-15] Pile-lined jacket, $30 [$20-25] Western hat, $15 [$10-15] Perma-prest® sport shirt, $4 [$10-12] Fall/winter 1981

Roebucks™ s-t-r-e-t-c-h denim jeans, $26 [$25-30] Western shirt, $14 [$10-15] Suede vest, $15 [$20-25] Spring/summer 1982

STRETCH ROEBUCKS™

"Authentic Western" stretch plaid shirt, $18 [$10-15] Stretch denim jeans, $24 [$25-35] Spring/summer 1982

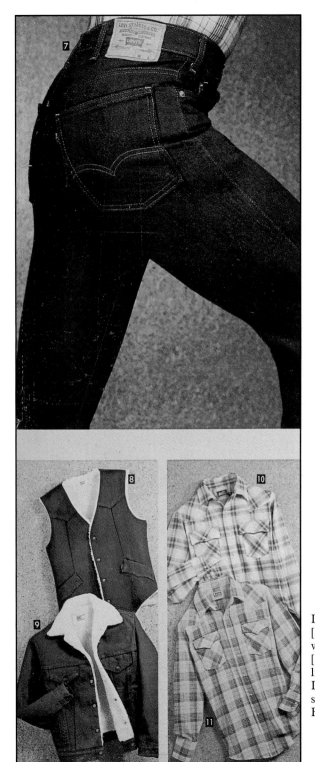

Levi's® stretch jeans, $30 [$60-80] Levi's® denim vest, pile lining, $40 [$15-20] Jacket with pile lining, $40 [$25-35] Levi's® yarn-dyed plaid shirts, $23 [$15-20] Fall/winter 1982

Sportswear

Feminine Fit

Sleeveless leotards, $9 [$5-10] Short-sleeved leotards, $10 [$5-10] Tights $4.50 [$2-5] Spring/summer 1980

Women dressed like ballerinas for their workouts up until the early 1980s. Some lingering styles shown here were used for the emerging aerobics fad. Assorted nylon leotards, $5-8 [$5-10] Tights, $2-4 [$2-5] Exercise shoes, vinyl on cotton knit backing, elasticized opening, $5 [$5-10] Spring/summer 1980

"Leotards that dazzle" in nylon and spandex, $15-18 [$5-10] Tank-style Unitard® with stirrup foot, $20 [$15-20] Spring/summer 1983

[9 thru 12] Leotards that dazzle
FABRIC, CARE: Sleek, comfortable Antron® nylon and
(11) Pinch front Leotard
. . . tank or long sleeved style
(12) New at Sears . . . the Unitard®

Ruffled tutu leotard, dotted leotard, Unitard™, $15-22 each [$5-20] Wrap 'n' tie skirt, $12 [$5-10] Leg warmers, $5.50 [$3-6] Fall/winter 1983

Color-coordinated active wear. Leotards, $14-16 [$5-10] Tights, $6 [$2-5] Shorts and skirt, $8-10 each [$5-15] Spring/summer 1983

104 ALL

Emerging Sports Stars

GO GOOLAGONG!

Tennis Panty

FABRIC, CARE: Specially knit opaque fabric with smooth nylon outside and cool, comfortable cotton inside. Cotton-lined crotch. Machine-wash, warm; tumble dry.
DETAIL: Elasticized waist. Pretty lace trim at legs.
ORDER INFO: Hip sizes 5(35-36); 6(37-38); 7(39-40) inches.
Store correct number size.
18 A 65999F—White
18 A 60181F—Fuchsia
18 A 60182F—Light blue
Shipping weight each 2 ounces.
Ea. $5.00...Any 2 or more, Ea. $4.75

Sears used sports stars for years to sell clothing — to men. But when Billy Jean King broke new ground for women, she helped pave the way for Evonne Goolagong's appearance on Sear's catalog pages. Warm-up jacket and pants, $35 [$15-20] Polo shirt, $15 [$5-10] Tank top, $10 [$5-10] Evonne Goolagong Tennis Shoe, $17 [$10-15] Spring/summer 1983

Long-sleeve top, $16 [$5-10] Polo top, $15 [$5-10] Pants, $15 [$5-10] Shorts, $12 [$5-10] Spring/summer 1983

Here the Wimbledon champion models active wear by Marilyn Kay. Shorts and skirt, $24 [$10-15] Spring/summer 1983

The Sweat Suit

In the late 1970s and early 1980s, everyone was jogging. The warm-up suit came into being, and became acceptable women's wear, from the sweatbands to the rapidly changing sneaker.

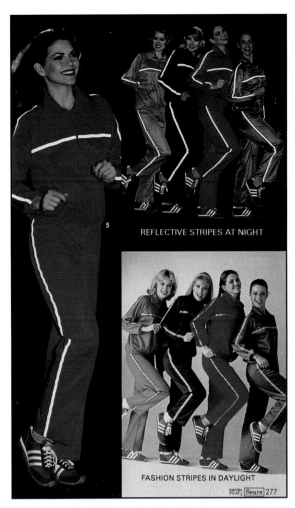

Separates. Colors are acrylic/cotton knit, grey items are acrylic, cotton and rayon with fleeced inside. Hooded sweatshirt, $12, racing shorts, $6, crew-neck sweatshirt, $8, and sweatpants, $10 [$5-15 each] Fall/winter 1980

Polyester knit jogging suit with reflective tape for nighttime safety, $38 [$10-15] Fall/winter 1980

Softly fleeced warm-up suit, $18 [$10-15] Fall/winter 1980

Fleeced coordinates. Crewneck sweatshirt, $9 [$5-10] Hooded sweatshirt, $9 [$5-10] Sweatpants, $11 [$5-10] Jogging shorts, $7 [$5-10] Striped V-neck top, $15 [$5-10] Spring/summer 1981

Heather gray sport coordinates for boys and teens, $6-10 each [$5-10 each] Spring/summer 1981

Color coordinated sportswear. Fashion sweatshirt, $13 [$10-15] V-neck top, $7 [$10-15] Coordinating shorts, $9 [$10-15] Spring/summer 1981

Active playwear for girls and pretty-plus sizes, $5-12 each [$5-10] Spring/summer 1981

Action mates. Zipper-front jacket, $17, pull-on shorts, $8, crew-neck top, $9, romper, $14 [$5-10 each] Spring/summer 1981

JUNIOR BAZAAR

TEAM UP WITH SUIT-YOUR-SPORT ™

122 Sears ALL

A new, sporty look — jogging shorts over sweatpants. Assorted separates: crewneck sweatshirt, $10, hooded sweatshirt, $14, jogging shorts, $8, and sweatpants, $12 [$5-15 each] Fall/winter 1981

Assorted separates: patterned crewneck top, $16, crewneck sweatshirt, $10, hooded sweatshirt, $14, jogging shorts, $8, and sweatpants, $12 [$5-15 each] Fall/winter 1981

Polyester knit separates, $10-18 each [$5-15] Spring/summer 1982

Fashion baseball-style jacket, $16 [$5-15]
Fall/winter 1981

Polyester/cotton warm-up suits, $25-29 [$15-20]
Turquoise warm-up separates, $15-20 [$5-10]
Spring/summer 1983

Kids were in on the exercising action, too. Here Disney tie-ins include Mousercise™ wear for infants and young children. Coordinates include leotards, tights, leg warmers, sweatshirt, and shoes, all designed for use with an exercise booklet and music. Spring/summer 1983

Exercising went co-ed in the early 1980s. Here his and hers warm-up suits from Wilson®, $26-28 [$30-35] Wilson® sweatshirts, sweatpants, and shorts, $10-20 [$15-20] Spring/summer 1983

Warm-up suits, polyester, nylon, and cotton, $35 [$20-25] Fall/winter 1983

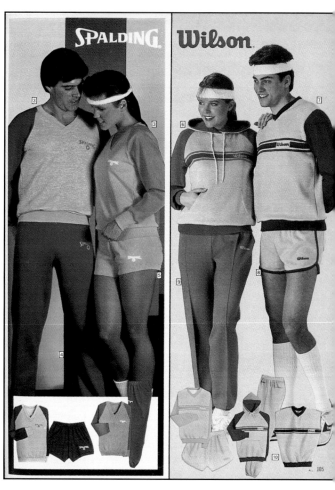

"Brand Name Sweat Separates for Men, Women," $13-22 [$10-15] Fall/winter 1983

His and hers Wilson warm-up suits, $28-$37 [$25-35] Fall/winter 1983

Scotchlite® Brand Reflective Fabric® trim on stripes and heel counter reflect bright silver-white light to help you be seen by motorist at night

The Winner II Runner

$18⁹⁹

Shoe (2) also available in narrow (N) sizes

"The Winner II Runner: nylon upper reinforced with suede, nylon tricot lining, padded tongue, sponge rubber insole, flared heel for shock absorbency, lightweight rubber sole, . . ." the sneaker goes high tech. $19 [$5-10] Spring/summer 1980

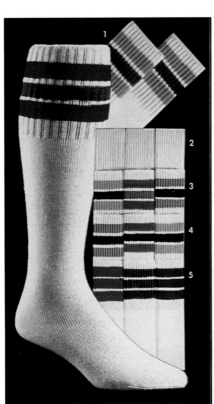

To go with the new sneakers, the sporty tube socks. These were worn, pulled up to the knee, with shorts. Three pairs, $3.50 [$2-5] Fall/winter 1980

The Running shoe for Men, Women and Big Boys

Designed to meet joggers' special needs . . . suitable for use as an all-around sports shoe

Men's sizes	Women's and Big Boys' sizes
$21⁹⁹	$20⁹⁹

All colors feature reflective fabric trim which reflects a bright silver-white light to help you be seen by approaching motorists at night.

Lightweight nylon and sueded split-leather upper

"Running shoe for men, women, and big boys," $21 [$10-15] Fall/winter 1980

Suddenly sport-specific shoes are born in a grab for market shares. You wore Converse® for basketball, Evonne Goolagong for tennis, Adidas® for jogging, . . . $16-44 [$30-50] Spring/summer 1983

Brand-name sneakers to "dazzle your competition," $18-40 [$30-50] Spring/summer 1983

116 ALL

Alternative Sports Style

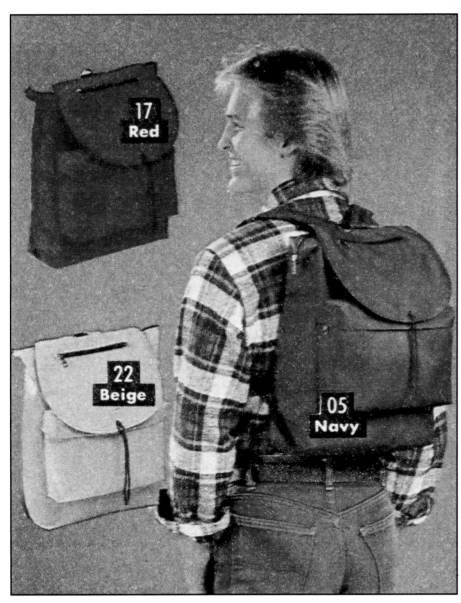

Back Pack-tote for the outdoorsey type, $8 [$5-10] Fall/winter 1980

Rugged leather boots for work or recreation, $54 [$40-50] Fall/winter 1980

**(1 thru 4)
Tough, durable
Hiking Boots have
leather construction**

Sueded split-leather
upper Hiking Boots
with leather lining or
warm acrylic pile lining
Your
choice $39⁹⁹

2 Smooth
leather
upper
Hiking Boots
$39⁹⁹

3 Sueded
split-leather
upper Hiking Boots
$29⁹⁹

4 Nylon and leather
upper Hiking Boots
$24⁹⁹

"Warm-lined boots for women who have rugged outdoor looks."
Suede upper with pile lining, $40 [$35-40] Smooth leather upper, 5
inches high, $40 [$35-40] Suede upper, $30 [$35-40] Nylon and
leather upper, $25 [$15-20] Fall/winter 1981

Lightweight Hiking Boots
with sueded split-leather
and nylon uppers

5

6

Lightweight hiking boots of nylon and suede on
rubber sole, $40 [$30-35] Fall/winter 1981

Swimwear

SPLASH WEAR

Left: Shirred-leg maillot, pull-on style, nylon and spandex, $19 [$15-20] Fashion sunglasses in fuchsia, burgundy, royal blue, or black, $16 [no value]. Spring/summer 1980

Right: Choose the top or bottom that fits you best, $8 each [$10-15] Spring/ summer 1980

Stretch-knit swimsuits in ruffle-edged, print, or crossover-front bikini styles, $14-18 [$25-35] Spring/summer 1980

Two-piece blouson swimsuit, solid or print, $19-21 [$20-30] Spring/summer 1981

Striped bikini in smooth-knit, $100, cotton, $15 [$30-40] Band-trimmed bikini, nylon/spandex knit, $18 [$25-35] Spring/summer 1980

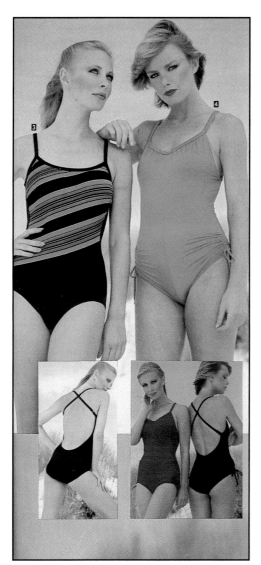

Print swimsuit with surplice effect plunging V-neckline, $26 [$15-25] Versatile print cover-up with elastic band on top, $22 [$10-15] Spring/summer 1981

Scoop-neck with multi-colored stripes, $16 [$20-30] Scoop-neck with adjustable side shirring, $20 [20-30] Spring/summer 1981

116 Sears ALL

Two-tone V-neck swim dress, lined inner bra and A-line skirt, elasticized panty, $26 [$40-50] Terry cover-up, $16 [$10-15] Spring/summer 1981

Vivid Swimwear

Flattering 2-piece swimsuits in misses' regular and full bust sizes and comfortable cover-up

Two-piece swimsuit with adjustable side ties, polyester knit, $15 [$25-35] Two-piece swim dress, smooth polyester knit, $17 [$15-20] Chenille cover-up, polyester and cotton, $17 [$10-15] Spring/summer 1981

Bandeau-style bikini with adjustable keyhole opening, $11, halter-style maillot, $11, and bandeau maillot with cut-out back, $11 [$15-25 each] Spring/summer 1981

Plunge-style maillot, $22 [$35-45] Bandeau-style maillot, $22 [$15-25] Textured nylon/spandex knit maillot, $22 [$25-35] Spring/summer 1981

THE MAILLOT

Floral bandeau maillot, $20, and scoop-neck maillot with adjustable shirring, $22 [$20-30 each] Spring/summer 1982

Bandeau print maillot, $20 [$15-25] V-neck maillot, $18 [$30-40] Spring/summer 1982

Print swimsuit with low-scooped back, inner bra, $28 [$20-30] Two-way print cover-up, $24 [$10-15] [$40-50 for set] Spring/summer 1982

22 Sears ALL

Body shaping swim dresses with figure control have hidden inner panel of spandex from under bust to top of panty, $25-30 [$35-45] Spring/summer 1982

Zip 'n' Tie "makes stylish terry cover-up and turns into a beach blanket with just one zip," in maize, light blue, white, or lilac, $20 [$10-15] Spring/summer 1982

INTRODUCING ZIP 'N TIE

Sold exclusively at Sears . . . great because it makes a stylish terry cover-up and also turns into a beach blanket with just one zip

$20 One size fits all

Sears ✳ Best

Ruffled maillot, $24 [$15-20] Tube bandeau with butterfly print, $20 [$15-20] Tonal color bikini with white floral print, $18 [$30-40] Spring/summer 1982

Blouson swimsuit, two-piece, $24 [$15-25] Mesh beach skimmer, $5 [$5-10] Spring/summer 1983

Footwear

Dress Shoes

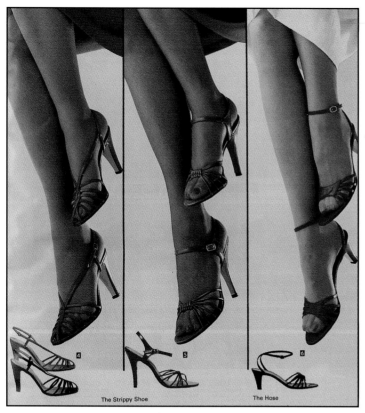

The Strippy Shoe   The Hose

Sling-back urethane sandal, $27 [$25-35] Instep strap sandal, $24 [$25-35] Sheer fashion pantyhose, $2.50 [$1-3] Spring/summer 1980

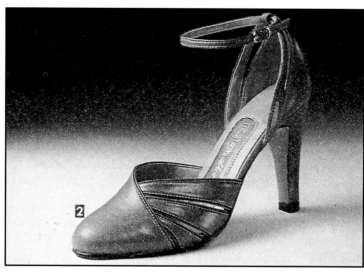

Shoe with open shank and side-slit vamp, $19 [$15-20] Fall/winter 1980

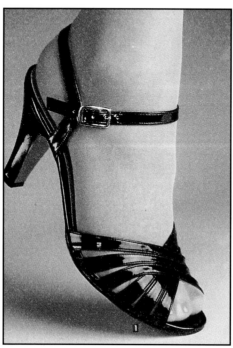

Sandal with "strippy" vamp, urethane, $19 [$15-20] Fall/winter 1980

Perforated sling, urethane upper,
$17 [$15-20] Convertible clutch,
$14 [$15-20 with shoes]
Spring/summer 1981

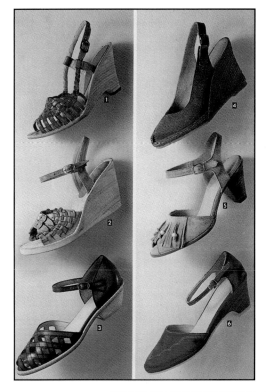

Leather-sandals. Woven upper, latticed
upper, suede pigskin sling, fringed and
beaded vamp, perfed and stitched vamp.
$20-22 each [$30-40] Fall/winter 1981

Pump with luster finish, open-toe woven
sandal, tassel pump, open-toe pump with
open shank, ankle strap sandal, $20 each
[$25-30] Fall/winter 1982

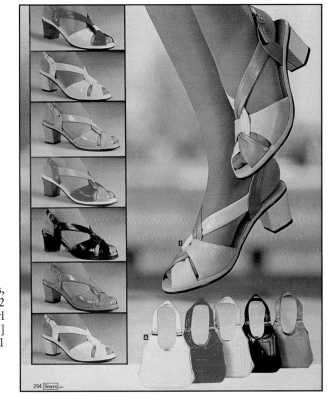

Fashion sandals,
urethane uppers, $12
[$15-30] Vinyl
handbag, $13 [$10-15]
Spring/summer 1981

Pigskin suede pump, spectator-style pump, sling pump, slip-on with tassel trim, and wedge sling with tassel trim, $18 each [$25-30] Urethane shoulder tote, $12 [$10-12] Fall/winter 1982

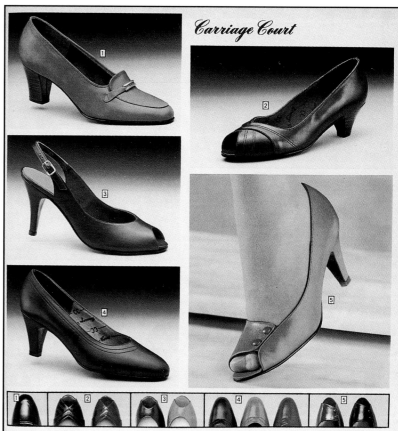

Carriage Court

Leather-upper pumps in five styles, $36 each [$30-40] Fall/winter 1983

Pantyhose in hound's-tooth, ribbed, sheer, lace, and opaque, $2.40 [$2-4] Fall/winter 1983

Casual

Fashion clogs, $19-24 each [$35-40] Spring/summer 1980

"Real moccasin construction" in squaw boot, beaded moccasin, kiltie-style wedge, and suede or smooth upper, $13-15 each [$25-35] Spring/summer 1981

Leather-upper casuals with textured bottoms, $27 each [$15-20] Fall/winter 1981

Soft knit heather-toned argyle, striped-calf, and striped knee highs, $1.70 per pair [$1-2] Fall/winter 1980

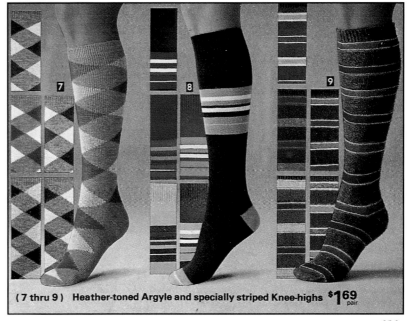

(7 thru 9)   Heather-toned Argyle and specially striped Knee-highs $1.69 pair

Fashion casuals with leather-like uppers, $20 each [$10-15] Fall/winter 1982

"Low-heeled, high-styled" casuals with leather uppers, $30 each [$15-20] Fall/winter 1983

Flats with leather or suede uppers, $25 [$25-30] Fall/winter 1983

Summer Sandals

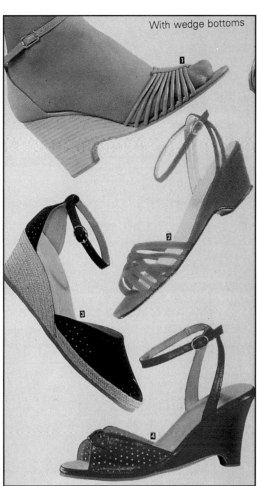

With wedge bottoms

Strippy sandal with stacked-look wedge heel, $17 [$20-30] Crossed-strip sandal, $15 [$15-20] Perforated Espadrille, $19 [$15-20] Bow-trim sandal, $16 [$15-20] Spring/summer 1981

Sandal with handwoven fabric upper, $16 [20-25] Spring/summer 1981

Leather-look casuals: T-strap, instep strap, or ankle strap, $19-20 each [$15-20] Spring/summer 1982

Thermal winter weather boots, waterproof with removable foam liner, $24 [$10-20] Fall/winter 1980

"Women's fashion boots" with leather-look urethane uppers, $28 each [$30-35]

Left: Leather-look boot with metallic-look trim, $35 [$15-20] Urethane boot with diamond-shaped overlay, $30 [$20-25] Urethane boot with decorative diamond shaft, $35 [$20-25] Western-stitched boot, $30 [$30-35] Fall/winter 1982

Right: "The latest in fashion . . . short casual boots, featuring smooth or sueded split leather, $40 or $30 [$25-30] Fall/winter 1983

Men's Shoes

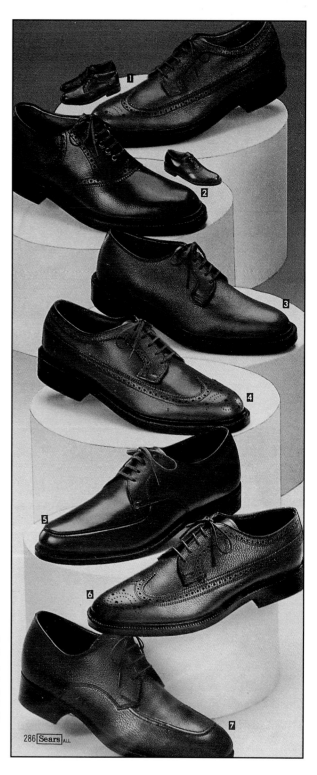

Levi's® leather or suede casuals for men. Hustler boot, $30 [$50-75] Camel tan moc-toe oxford, 3-eyelet tie oxford, and Tempest Oxford, $40 each [$50-75] Slip on with penny saddle, $50 [$50-75] Walker II sport Oxford, $50 [$35-50] Dusty athletic Oxford, $33 [$50-70] Spring/summer 1981

All-leather brogues and saddle Oxford, $60 [$70-75] Leather-upper Oxfords with man-made soles, rubber heels, $40 [$40-50] Leather-upper Oxfords with PVC unit sole and heel, $30 [$40-50] Spring/summer 1982

Outer Wear

Casual

Colorful nylon ciré zip-jacket, $15 [$15-20] Spring/summer 1980

Action jackets, water-repellent and hooded for added protection. Reversible slicker of PVC vinyl, $15 [$25-35] Smooth poplin shirt-jacket, polyester and cotton, $20 [$20-25] Nylon jogging jacket, $12 [$15-25] Spring/summer 1980

. . . fiberfill-lined to keep warmth in; cold out. Machine washable.

SLEEVES ZIP-OFF . . .
JACKET CONVERTS
TO VEST

Jacket with zip-off sleeves, collar converts to turtle-neck, $35 [$15-20] Fall/winter 1980

Stroller of acrylic and modacrylic pile, looks like mink, $100 [$110-125] Fall/winter 1980

Some colors
ALSO IN TALL

Some Jackets
ALSO IN EXTRA TALL

(1 thru 6)   You'll like these Jackets and Vests away from the slopes

"You'll like these jackets and vests away from the slopes." Jackets, $50 [$30-40] Vests, $35
[$20-30] Fall/winter 1980

Sportcoat of modacrylic and acrylic pile, looks like feathered mink, $90 [$120-135]
Fall/winter 1980

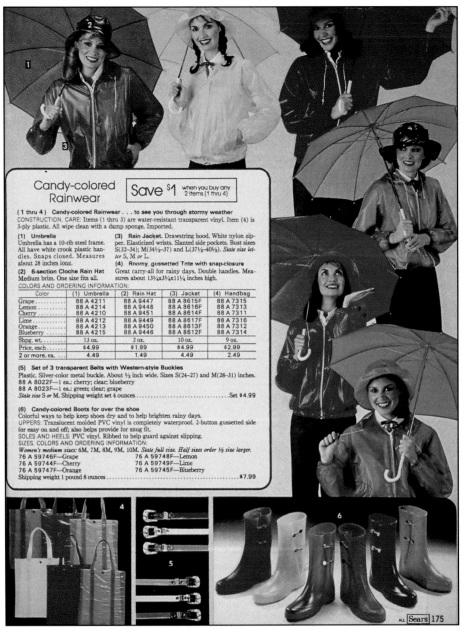

Candy colored rainwear. Umbrella, $5 [$5-7] 6-section cloche rain hat, $2 [$3-5] Rain jacket, drawstring hood, $5 [$5-10] Spring/summer 1981

REAL FUR

Wrap jacket of full-skin rabbit, $169 [$150-200] Blazer jacket of rabbit, $129 [$150-200] Designer look jacket of natural sectioned opossum, $249 [$200-230] Fall/winter 1981

ALL Sears 135

Zip-off hooded jacket, polyester/cotton poplin shell, nylon and polyester linings; poplin shell, nylon/polyester lining, corduroy inner collar, $50; poplin jacket with plaid lining, $50 each [$40-50] Fall/winter 1981

Pile-lined parkas with nylon, taffeta outer shell, $48 [$15-20] Fall/winter 1981

The Leather Shop

(1) Grain cowhide Jacket with warm acrylic pile zip-out liner for 3-season wear

$89⁹⁹ Regular sizes

FABRIC: Grain cowhide shell. Smooth nylon body and sleeve lining. Zip-out liner is soft acrylic pile with cotton backing.

DETAIL: Zip front. Straight front and back yokes. Diagonal stitching and welted pockets give a fashionable look. Set-in sleeves. Regular sizes about 24 inches long. Imported.

CARE: Professionally leather clean. Dry clean zip-out liner.

SIZES, COLORS, ORDER INFO: Shipped on a hanger. See Shipping Note, page 589.

Regular. For men over 5 ft. 7 in. to 5 ft. 11 in. tall. *State even chest size* 36, 38, 40, 42, 44 or 46.
N 45 G 62931F—Tan
N 45 G 62932F—Cordovan
N 45 G 62933F—Black
Shpg. wt. 2 lbs. 5 oz. $89.99

Tall. For men over 5 ft. 11 in. to 6 ft. 3 in. tall. *State even chest size* 38, 40, 42, 44 or 46.
N 45 G 62941F—Tan
N 45 G 62943F—Black
Shpg. wt. 2 lbs. 9 oz. $99.99

Extra Tall. For men over 6 ft. 3 in. to 6 ft. 7 in. tall. *State even chest size* 40, 42, 44, 46 or 48.
N 45 G 62951F—Tan
Shpg. wt. 2 lbs. 11 oz. $109.99

Big-Tall. For men over 5 ft. 11 in. to 6 ft. 3 in. tall. *State even chest size* 48, 50 or 52.
N 45 G 62961F—Tan
Shpg. wt. 2 lbs. 11 oz. $109.99

ALSO IN TALL
(1) Also in **EXTRA TALL, BIG-TALL**

(2) Grain cowhide Jacket with smooth nylon lining

$79⁹⁹ Regular sizes

FABRIC: Grain cowhide shell. Nylon body and sleeve lining.

DETAILING: Zip front. Panel front with half-waistband. Pointed yokes front and back. Set-in double welt pockets. Set-in sleeves. Regular sizes about 24 inches long. Imported.

CARE: Professionally leather clean.

SIZES, COLORS. ORDER INFO: Shipped on a hanger. See Shipping Note, page 589.

Regular. For men over 5 ft. 7 in. to 5 ft. 11 in. tall. *State even chest size* 36, 38, 40, 42, 44 or 46.
N 45 G 62304F—Tan
N 45 G 62305F—Brown
Shpg. wt. 2 lbs. 3 oz. $79.99

Tall. For men over 5 ft. 11 in. to 6 ft. 3 in. tall. *State even chest size* 38, 40, 42, 44 or 46.
N 45 G 62314F—Tan
Shpg. wt. 2 lbs. 6 oz. $89.99

Just call Sears and say "Charge It" . . . see page 679

ALL Sears 585

Grain cowhide jacket with acrylic pile zip-out liner, $90 [$150-175] Cowhide jacket with smooth nylon lining, $80 [$110-130] Fall/winter 1981

Rugged wear

Zip off sleeves and **it's a vest . . .** zip on sleeves and **it's a jacket**

100 Sears ALL

Convertible jacket-vest with zip-on sleeves, $50 [$30-40] Fall/winter 1982

Wrap-styled rabbit jacket with wing collar, soft suede tie belt, $129 [$110-135] Tailored rabbit blazer with cardigan front, one button, $109 [$110-135] Fall/winter 1983

Jackets with sport striping and corduroy trim, nylon shell, polyester fiberfill, $35 [$20-30] Fall/winter 1983

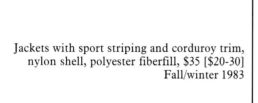

The Balmacaan, poplin of polyester and cotton, treated for shower resistance, water-repellent nylon lining, zip-in lining, in peanut tan, navy, or natural, $43 [$50-60] Double-brreasted trench of woven polyester, treated for shower resistance, nylon lining, $30 [$35-45] Spring/summer 1980

THE GREAT TRENCH

Superbly tailored poplin rainclassic comes with or without zip-out liner. Trenchcoat features include: epaulets, sleeve straps and a buckled belt long enough to tie. Coat and liner are machine washable.

A wardrobe essential and low priced at

Misses' sizes **$55** Without Zip-liner

ZIP-LINED VERSION, TALL MISSES' AND HALF SIZES PRICED HIGHER

Zip-lined version has 34-in. long pile liner ... the longest liner we sell

Top-stitching accents the trench detailing

Front and back rainshield-flaps give added protection

Buttons are shank-wrapped for sturdiness

Trenchcoat with epaulets, sleeve straps, and a buckled belt long enough to tie, poplin with zip-out liner, $70 [$60-75] Spring/summer 1980

Also in Petite Misses' and Tall Misses' sizes

Also in Petite Misses' and Half sizes

Also in Petite Misses' Tall Misses', Half and Women's sizes

Double-breasted wool fleece coat, $130 [$80-100] Scarf coat in wool/polyester-blend tweed, $95 [$50-75] Full coat in wool/rayon blend fleece, $110 [$60-70] Fall/winter 1981

Styles 2 and 3 Also in Petite and Tall Misses' and Half sizes

Full-length leather coat with detachable lamb's fur collar dyed to look like raccoon, zip-out pile liner, $220 [$180-225] Full-length tailored leather coat, zip-out pile liner, $195 [$180-200] Fall/winter 1980

All-weather coats of shower resistant poplin in three styles: Balmacaan or trenchcoat, $65 each [$40-55], or the topper, $45 [$25-35] Spring/summer 1982

Double-breasted coat in camel hair/wool/nylon blend, satin acetate lining, $170 [$100-150] Fall/winter 1982

Down-filled coat with vertical quilting, scalloped stitching, high shawl collar, $168 [$80-100] Cowhide leather jackets with acetate satin lining in blouson or blazer styles, $153 [$175-200] Fall/winter 1982

Trenchcoat with leather buttons, D-ring trim, $128 [$35-50] Flared coat with zip-out liner for warmth, demi-belted back, $77 [$35-50] Fall/winter 1982

147

Smooth cowhide leather coats with zip-out pile liners in full-length tailored style, $202-232 [$180-200] With detachable lamb's fur collar, $228-258 [$180-210] Fall/winter 1982

Quilted cowhide jacket with woven nylon lining, polyester fiberfill, $133 [$75-80] Fall/winter 1982

Flared coat in soft wool with acetate taffeta lining, $98 [$80-100] Polyester plush coat with rabbit fur collar, acetate taffeta lining, $105 [$80-90] Fall/winter 1982

Shower-resistant polyester and cotton poplin coat with burgundy leather, acetate lining, double-breasted snap closure, $80 [$55-65] Spring/summer 1983

Leather piped raincoat or polyester/cotton poplin, zip-out Thinsulate® liner, $95 [$90-110] Down-filled coat, polyester/nylon shell, nylon lining, $180 [$90-110] Fall/winter 1983

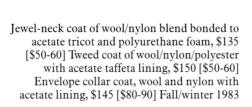

Jewel-neck coat of wool/nylon blend bonded to acetate tricot and polyurethane foam, $135 [$50-60] Tweed coat of wool/nylon/polyester with acetate taffeta lining, $150 [$50-60] Envelope collar coat, wool and nylon with acetate lining, $145 [$80-90] Fall/winter 1983

Plush reefer coat, wool and nylon bonded to acetate and polyurethane foam, $110 [$60-75] Hooded coat with plaid scarf, wool, nylon, and other man-made fibers, acetate lining, $105 [$60-75] Plush coat with fur-look collar, $80 [$60-75] Fall/winter 1983

Down-filled coat with stand-up collar, slanted front and back yokes, $160 [$90-110] Down-filled coat with convertible collar, $160 [$90-110] Fall/winter 1983

Leather blazer, nylon lining, $100-130 [$150-175] Fall/winter 1983

Nightwear

Nightwear and lounge wear changed remarkably in the 1980s. Leaving behind the charming robes that served as hostess gowns the previous decade, lounge wear transformed into slick, shiny, and skimpy styles. The sexual revolution had come to fruition, and the lounge wear of the 1980s made no pretentions of innocence.

Print and Solid Tricot Nightwear

172 Sears ALL

Shimmering and sleek wrap robe and sleepwear: floral coat, $25 [$10-15], slip-on floral or solid gown, $18 [$10-15], mini pajama, $15 [$15-20] Spring/summer 1980

NIGHT GLAMOUR

A little lace here
a little slit there
a splash of regal
grape and the
results are
so soft ... so sleek
... so sensuous

TALL SIZES ALSO
AVAILABLE IN
STYLES 1 AND 3

"Satin boudoir slide," $12 [$10-15] Pullover gown with keyhole opening, $17 [$25-30]
Slip-style gown, $15 [$25-30] Long wrap coat, $24 [$20-25] "Short 'n' sassy mini pajama,
$15 [$10-15] Fall/winter 1980

SLEEK

Our fine quality
knit nightwear
features sharp
detailing and
lavish trim

$13.00 average sizes

Long, lavishly
gathered gown with
two-tie option, $13
[$10-15] Fitted gown,
$13 [$15-20] Jumpsuit,
$13 [$10-15] Slip gown
with double spaghetti
straps, $13 [$10-15]
Fall/winter 1980

ALL Sears 397

153

Candy-striped Plissé

FABRIC AND CARE: Polyester and cotton plissé. Machine wash, warm; tumble dry.
DETAILING: Banded wrap style with matching sash to tie at waist. Pretty piping adds fashion flair. Side-seam pocket.
SIZES, COLORS AND ORDERING INFORMATION:
Average . . . fits 5 ft. 3 in. to 5 ft. 6½ in. Misses' sizes S(8-10); M(12-14); L(16-18).

Ankle-length style with ¾-length sleeves
State letter size S, M or L from above.
38 A 68212F—Blue and white stripe
38 A 68211F—Pink and white stripe
Shipping weight 15 ounces........$18.00

Knee-length style with short sleeves
State letter size S, M or L from above.
38 A 68202F—Blue and white stripe
38 A 68201F—Pink and white stripe
Shipping weight 11 ounces........$16.00

ALL Sears 207

Ankle length sleep/lounge wear, $18 [$25-30] Knee-length, $16 [$20-25] Spring/summer 1981

Night Glamour

Alluring décolleté and extravagant lace trim for a look that's feminine and fabulous

TALL SIZES ALSO AVAILABLE

"Alluring long gown," $19 [$10-15] Elegant wrap coat, $26 [$15-20] Tunic-top pajama, $20 [$15-20] Wispy mini-pajama, $18 [$10-15] Spring/summer 1981

Pajama with button-front top, pants, $14 [$15-20] Wrap-style coat, $15 [$15-20] Slip-style gown, $11 [$10-15] Mini-length gown, $10 [$10-15] Spring/summer 1981

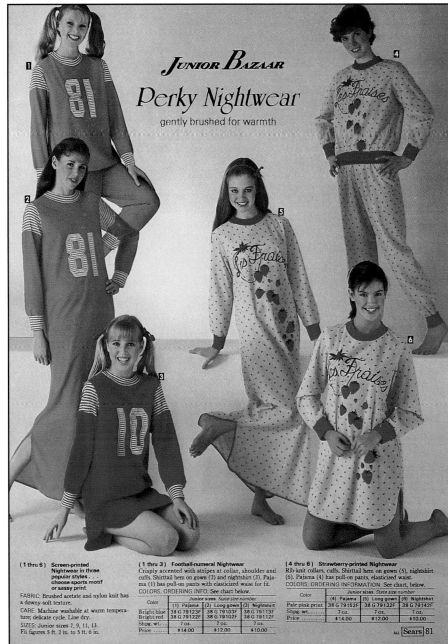

Junior Bazaar

Perky Nightwear
gently brushed for warmth

(1 thru 6) Screen-printed Nightwear in three popular styles . . . choose sports motif or sassy print
FABRIC: Brushed acetate and nylon knit has a downy-soft texture.
CARE: Machine washable at warm temperature; delicate cycle. Line dry.
SIZES: Junior sizes 7, 9, 11, 13.
Fit figures 5 ft. 2 in. to 5 ft. 6 in.

(1 thru 3) Football-numeral Nightwear
Crisply accented with stripes at collar, shoulder and cuffs. Shirttail hem on gown (2) and nightshirt (3). Pajama (1) has pull-on pants with elasticized waist for fit.
COLORS, ORDERING INFO: See chart below.

Color	Junior sizes. *State size number*		
	(1) Pajama	(2) Long gown	(3) Nightshirt
Bright blue	38 G 79123F	38 G 79103F	38 G 79113F
Bright red	38 G 79122F	38 G 79102F	38 G 79112F
Shpg. wt.	7 oz.	7 oz.	7 oz.
Price	$14.00	$12.00	$10.00

(4 thru 6) Strawberry-printed Nightwear
Rib-knit collars, cuffs. Shirttail hem on gown (5), nightshirt (6). Pajama (4) has pull-on pants, elasticized waist.
COLORS, ORDERING INFORMATION: See chart, below.

Color	Junior sizes. *State size number*		
	(4). Pajama	(5) Long gown	(6) Nightshirt
Pale pink print	38 G 79152F	38 G 79132F	38 G 79142F
Shpg. wt.	7 oz.	7 oz.	7 oz.
Price	$14.00	$12.00	$10.00

Football numeral nightwear, $10-14 [$15-20] Strawberry print nightwear, $10-14 [$15-20] Fall/winter 1981

Flannel nightwear: gown with keyhole opening, ruffled yoke, $14 [$10-15], wrap coat, $20 [$10-15], cullotte, $16 [$10-15], two styles of pajamas with and without feet, $16-19 [$15-20] Fall/winter 1981

"Take-alongs for lounging . . . travel," crepe-texture nylon knit. Ankle- or full-length print and full-length pastel zip-front, $18-20 [$25-30] Wrap style, ankle or knee length, $22 [$20-25] Spring/summer 1982

Perma-prest® polyester and cotton nightwear. Knee-length wrap coat, $17 [$15-20] Ankle-length wrap coat, $21 [$15-20] Ankle-length gown with spaghetti straps, $16 [$15-20]. Mini pajama, $13 [$15-20] Spring/summer 1982

Satin triacetate and nylon robe and lounging pajama, $20 and $24 [$35-40] Fall/winter 1983

Cotton/polyester quilted robe, knee and ankle length, $19 and $22 [$20-25] Terry wrap robe, $21 [$30-35] Terry print lounge gown, $10 [$10-15] Fall/winter 1982

"Glamourous sleepwear with metallic shimmer and lace." Lacy camisole and knickers, $14 [$15-20] Gown and wrap coat, $22 [$30-35] Mini peignoir, $13 [$20-25] Long peignoir, $28 [$30-35] Fall/winter 1982

Terry knit snap-front robe, $27 [$30-35] Mini- and ankle-length wrap robes, $22 and $26 [$10-15] Striped mini wrap, $15 [$10-15] Zip-front lounging robe with garden print, $24 [$15-20] Spring/summer 1983

"Inspirations from Yesteryear." Lacy stretch teddy briefer, $20 [$30-35] Four-way teddy briefer, with or without straps, halter style, or with straps crossed in back, $23 [$30-35] Fall/winter 1983

"Lustrous satin for at-home glamour." Zip-front robe, with ruffles at neck and wrists, $23 [$10-15]
Wrap robe, $21 [$20-25] Lounging pajama, $22 [$15-20] Fall/winter 1983